RESPECTFUL
PARENTS
Respectful
Kids

RESPECTFUL PARENTS
Respectful
Kids

7 Keys to Turn Family Conflict Into Co-operation

Sura Hart and Victoria Kindle Hodson

PuddleDancer
PRESS

P.O. Box 231129, Encinitas, CA 92023-1129
email@PuddleDancer.com ▪ www.PuddleDancer.com

PuddleDancer Press, Permissions Dept.
P.O. Box 231129, Encinitas, CA 92023-1129
Fax: 1-858-759-6967, email@PuddleDancer.com

Authors: Sura Hart and Victoria Kindle Hodson

Illustrator: Martin Mellein, MGM Graphic Design

Book Design: Lightbourne, Inc.

Manufactured in the United States of America

1st Printing, October 2006

10 9 8 7 6 5 4 3

ISBN 10: 1-892005-22-0

ISBN 13: 978-1-892005-22-9

Advance Praise for *Respectful Parents, Respectful Kids*

"This exceptional book is the 'deepest dive' I've ever found in cultivating genuine mutual respect between parents and children. The *7 Keys* provide specific, well-documented exercises and practical strategies that address family challenges, opening doors that are often closed, and give everyone the freedom to really enjoy one another."

—STEPHEN R. COVEY, author, *The 7 Habits of Highly Effective People* and *The 8th Habit: From Effectiveness to Greatness*

"Many parents won't give up punishment because they think the only alternative is permissiveness. Other parents don't understand the long-term dangers of permissiveness, but they sure don't want to be punitive. This delightful book shows parents how to get the best results for their children with respectful parenting tools that are neither punitive nor permissive."

—JANE NELSEN, Ed.D., co-author of *the Positive Discipline series*

"Gandhi advised us to 'become the change we want to see in the world.' *Respectful Parents, Respectful Kids* brings this time-honored wisdom up to date with simple, life-changing exercises. Know thyself. Communicate clearly, nonviolently, with purpose and respect and that is exactly how your children will treat you. This marvelous book shows you how."

—MICHAEL MENDIZZA, Touch the Future, founder of the Nurturing Project

"After decades of teaching and raising a large family, I can say with enthusiasm that Hart and Hodson have it right. This is a practical, generous, supportive, and loving book. A major help to parents."

—NEL NODDINGS, Ph.D., author, *Educating Moral People* and *Starting at Home: Caring and Social Policy*

"Refreshing, insightful, and informative, this book provides a long-awaited alternative to outdated parenting paradigms that are not satisfying for parents or kids. It helps parents focus on what is most important to them, and create deeper and more meaningful connections with their children. This is the best parent read since *How To Talk So Kids Will Listen*!"

—BRENDA HARARI, Ph.D., HEART in Education

"Articulate, practical, fun and extraordinarily insightful, this book is destined to become the new manual in parent/child relationships. More than theory, the seven keys are real-life tools for creating more joyful, cooperative, loving interactions with our children: a must-read, must-do guide without question!"

—RESA STEINDEL BROWN, author, *The Call to Brilliance*

"I have practiced conflict resolution as a divorce attorney and mediator for 31 years. *Respectful Parents, Respectful Kids* gives me the first parenting book I can offer to clients confident that it will help heal the family pain and destruction from which they seek relief."

—STEVEN ALLEN SMITH, mediator and divorce attorney

"Superbly written and easy to read, *Respectful Parents, Respectful Kids* is a powerful and practical guide for parents everywhere. For those of you who long for more cooperation, mutual respect, trust, and harmony within the family, this book offers concrete useful tools that will help you immediately begin this transformation."

—LISA LIFRAK, MFT, marriage and family therapist

"We wish that we had the tools that we learned in this book when we first became parents 14 years ago. This book can give parents the confidence, language and skills to be the kind of parent they always wanted to be: understanding, compassionate, respectful and fun."

—CARLA ADIVI, parent and middle school teacher

"*Respectful Parents, Respectful Kids* provides a valuable tool for parents to generate deeper compassion and connection. It will be a valuable addition to the Nonviolent Communication training I offer to my private clientele worldwide."

—SUSAN ALLAN, America's leading Marriage and Divorce Coach, and certified mediator

This book is dedicated to children—here to show us how to live with honesty, curiosity, vulnerability, courage, authenticity, and exuberance.

And, especially, to Brian, Kyra, and Marieka.

Contents

Charts & Activities

Charts

Family Activities

Topic: Giraffe & Jackal Culture

Topic: Family Meetings

Topic: Life-Enriching Practices

Topic: Peaceful Conflict Resolution

Topic: Giraffe & Jackal Play

Preface

In 2003 we wrote *The Compassionate Classroom: Relationship Based Teaching and Learning.* In that book our goal was to share with teachers a "no-fault" mode of communicating developed by Dr. Marshall B. Rosenberg and known as Nonviolent Communication, or NVC for short. We were motivated to write *The Compassionate Classroom* because it is a book that we wish had existed when we were classroom teachers searching for effective ways to create with our students the co-operative learning environment that we knew must be possible somehow. Since the publication of *The Compassionate Classroom,* we have been very gratified to hear from teachers in different parts of the world that the book has helped them to make their classrooms into relationship based learning environments.

Now we find ourselves once again writing a book together to share NVC, this time with parents. We have been parenting longer than we have been teaching, so for us the themes we discuss and write about in this book strike even deeper chords of recognition and stir many memories from when we were young parents. While the core parenting themes that we address in this book are much the same as those we remember experiencing in the 1970s when our children were young, we realize that much has changed in the culture in the last twenty-five years and that those changes make parenting more complex and challenging now than perhaps ever before.

Thinking back to when we were new parents, we are grateful that we were able to spend the first few years at home with our children. In the 1960s and 1970s it was more possible for one salary to support a middle-class family. And while parenting was not quite considered "real work," it was generally accepted that middle-class mothers would stay home with their babies. Some industrialized nations today support mothers who stay home with their children for the first three years; however, here in the United States not only is there no government support for that choice, but the average cost of living now requires two working parents to support a middle-class standard of living for a family.

Along with economic stress, families today are feeling the stress of the increasing speed of life and the rush of information delivered by high-speed technologies such as the Internet, e-mail, instant messaging, and cell phones. We are able to do much more than before and do it faster—so we are multi-tasking like crazy in order to do as much and get as much as we possibly can. Technology was supposed to make us freer to spend more time with family, hobbies, and recreation. Instead we have created new standards for what is possible to achieve and higher expectations for super-companies, super-employees, super-moms and -dads, and super-kids. People's emotional reactions have also speeded up, and even small glitches, delays, or detours can set us off. Emotional overload added to mental overload can drain our energy and make us tired and cranky.

In response to the above "bad news," this book brings good news about a proven approach to respectful interpersonal communication that families are using to address and meet the needs of every family member and to transform conflict into co-operation. In writing this book, we hope to support you in choosing how you parent based on your deepest values and what you most want for your children.

Acknowledgements

We would like to acknowledge, with deep appreciation, the following contributors to this book:

Our Collaborators
Our primary editors Kyra Freestar and Stan Hodson, who spent days and nights reading, shaping, and giving continuity to this manuscript.

Our illustrator Marty Mellein, for his understanding and his support for this project as well as for his ability to make a drawing say a thousand words.

Meiji Stewart and Neill Gibson from PuddleDancer Press, who for many years have held the vision to publish a parenting book and who made this opportunity possible. We admire and appreciate their willingness and ability to live the NVC process in their business practices. We would also like to thank Tiffany Meyer and Shannon Bodie, members of the PuddleDancer team, for their flexibility, availability, and unwavering support.

Our Teachers
The parents who have studied and consulted with us over the years and who gave us the courage to write this book in the first place.

Marshall B. Rosenberg, for creating and sharing the process of Nonviolent Communication that is at the heart of *Respectful Parents, Respectful Kids*.

J. Krishnamurti, whose work brought us together in 1986 to teach at his school in Ojai, California. Talks with him took us to new depths of understanding about concepts such as thought, fear, and human motivation for action and paved the way for our understanding and embracing Nonviolent Communication.

Foreword

It's been quite some time since my child-rearing years, and yet nearly every day parents in my workshops all around the world come to me expressing their pain and challenges in raising their children. The challenges are definitely familiar to me, yet the demands of today's overbooked schedules and the influences from the outside world are far more disquieting than ever before. Every day thousands of messages of violence and mistrust reach our children. In addition, there is the overwhelming pressure to define ourselves by what we have rather then what we value, and confused parents are crying out for help and support. It is time that we answered their call.

Respectful Parents, Respectful Kids comes as a compelling answer to this call at a vitally important time—when perhaps never before has the foundation of the family been more important to the future of our society and the well being of our planet. The tools in this book empower parents to serve as effective, active forces for change in families, communities, and the larger world. I agree with the authors when they say, "The way you parent will affect not only your child, but the lives of hundreds and perhaps thousands of people in your child's future. You don't have a choice about whether or not to affect this net of interdependence; however, you do have a choice about *how* you affect it."

Authors Sura Hart and Victoria Kindle Hodson go beyond quick-fix parenting and disciplinary techniques and provide a foundation of communication and relationship skills that dramatically improve the quality of parent-child relationships. With the help of this book, parents become skilled at transforming habitual communication patterns that are out of harmony with their desire to contribute to their child's development. And by practicing these essential skills, parents can establish an emotionally safe and supportive environment where children can reach their fullest potential.

We are all born into this world with an inherent sense of our interconnectedness and a need for community and support. We are also born with a natural sense of compassion. However, it is our experiences—those moments when our needs are not respected in homes, schools, and organizations—that tarnish these natural states and turn us instead to meeting our needs through "power-over" tactics such as demands, coercion, and other violent behaviors. Or worse yet, we forget that our needs matter at all.

Respectful Parents, Respectful Kids provides a new way of understanding children's behavior, and a new way of responding to it. When you use the tools provided in this book, you will build a foundation of trust with your children. Children who have the support of a home environment where trust thrives—where their needs are respected—are much more likely to lead healthy, productive lives. This foundation of trust is the beginning of strong self-esteem, and the basis of the mutual respect and loving connection parents everywhere want with their children.

In this very practical and deeply important book you can learn the tools and skills you need to truly prepare your children for the world. Regardless of where they are destined to go, you can send them off emotionally literate and conscious of their interconnectedness with others. By creating a home where trust thrives and where all needs are respected, you will empower your children to discover their potential, and to become lifelong contributors to the future of their families, their communities, and our planet.

Do more than read this book. Live these principles. Share them with your spouse, your friends, and your children. One parent and one household at a time, we will create a world where all needs are met peacefully.

Marshall B. Rosenberg, Ph.D.

Founder and educational director of the Center for Nonviolent Communication
Author of *Nonviolent Communication: A Language of Life,*
Speak Peace in a World of Conflict, and *Raising Children Compassionately*

Introduction

This book is offered in the conviction that parenting is one of the most important, most rewarding, and most demanding activities that human beings ever undertake. With an emphasis on creating respect and co-operation between parents and children, the book introduces 7 keys to unlock and inspire specific parenting capacities. These capacities include parenting with a purpose clearly in mind, looking beyond behavior to the needs that motivate it, and actively choosing structures and practices that fulfill one's purposes and intentions.

We still vividly remember our younger selves as new moms in our twenties, mothers of grade-school children in our thirties, and mothers of high-schoolers in our forties. During all of those times, we wanted more understanding, clarity, and support for our parenting. What we were then experiencing ran counter to society's prevailing notions of parenting. We were seeing an integrity and wholeness in our children that we wanted to interact with, marvel at, and learn from. We saw possibilities for growing with our children, learning together, and coming to deeper understandings of the world through our interactions with them. At that time in the 1970s and 1980s, most support for parents did not focus on ways to reduce family conflict and enjoy being with children but instead promoted ways to manage conflict by managing kids' behavior.

This behavior management approach to parenting persists today. Hundreds of books and articles are published each year that direct parents to get kids to do what they want them to do through guilt, shame, praise, fear of punishment, or promise of rewards. In recent decades the approach has softened a bit. Terms that are currently being used, such as natural consequences, time-outs, and positive incentives, sound friendlier, but the end goal is still the same—to control kids' behavior.

Most parents we know have tried at least a few of these managerial approaches and have found them less than satisfying. Although the tips and methods sometimes help them get more of the kind of behavior they want and do reduce conflict for a while, the gains are always short-term and always come at great cost. The more these parents have tried to manage their kids' behavior by laying down the law, imposing consequences, and motivating with rewards, the more power struggles, yelling matches, slammed doors, icy stares, and tears they experienced. Many parents tell us that these behavior management approaches are difficult to carry out because they go against their parenting instincts and their desire to create goodwill and heartfelt connections with their kids.

What You Live Is What They Learn

Respectful Parents, Respectful Kids offers a refreshing alternative to managerial parenting. The good news is: you don't have to figure out how to change your kids' behavior, and you don't have to *manage* anything, in order to end conflicts. The parenting we advocate is in many ways much simpler and more instinctive than this. It is also more effective in meeting the needs of kids and parents, in the short term and, especially, in the long term. It builds on the good feelings you and your children experience at your most connected moments, and it addresses the only behavior you can actually change—your own. The beauty of it is, when you change your behavior, your kids' behavior will change too.

It is commonly believed that a parent's job is to teach and enforce cultural values. Customary methods for doing this include lecturing, advising, making demands, and correcting behavior. This parent-as-teacher orientation is, unfortunately, a set-up that creates frustrated parents, irritated children, and conflict all around. At the same time that you are doing your best to teach your kids cultural values, they are doing their best to develop a sense of self-direction and self-respect. All too often they learn to turn a deaf ear to you and your advice. They avoid saying anything that might result in another lecture, admonishment, or ultimatum that reminds them how they are failing to live up to your expectations.

As a parent, of course you want to have influence with your children; you want to pass on values and guide them in ways that will contribute to their happiness and success in life. The question is: How can you have the most influence with your children—by lecturing and taking them to task or by sharing your values and living those values yourself?

Everyone knows that actions speak louder than words. In fact, studies show that only 5 percent of lifelong learning comes from instruction: 95 percent of what we remember comes from family and social interactions.[1] At some level you likely know that your children learn more from what you do than from what you say. You may hear your own voice in the way one sibling talks with another. You may hear your children using the same line of reasoning with you that you use with them.

Think for a moment about what you learned from your parents. Did you learn the most from, or even listen to half of, what they told you? Or did you learn the most from what you saw them do and how they lived their lives? Many parents tell us that they learned from painful experiences with their parents what they *didn't* want to do with their own kids. Whether their modeling was positive or negative, your parents' actions are a primary motivating force for the way you are parenting and the life you are living now.

Children need parents who live honestly and with commitment to their values. Parents have a chance to be exemplars and model what they want their children to learn and live. This is an invitation and opportunity, and for many it is a powerful incentive to get clear about what has purpose and meaning for them and to do their best to live in harmony with it.

To live authentically, with clarity about what is important and true for you, is the goal—not perfection. Giving up the ideal of being a perfect parent can be a huge relief. Then, when you blow it and do things that don't match your values—as you will—you won't spiral down into self-condemnation but will be able to enjoy the opportunity to be honest with your children and let them learn what honesty looks and sounds

---

1. Mendizza and Pearce, *Magical Parent, Magical Child.*

like. And because you aren't expecting perfection from yourself, you will be less likely to expect it from your children.

Build Your Capacity to Create a Loving Home

Your home is where your children learn the most elemental lessons of human life—how to take care of their own needs and how to contribute to taking care of the needs of others. Home is a foundation for your children's future relationships as spouses, life partners, mothers, fathers, aunts, uncles, grandmothers, grandfathers, good friends, community members, co-workers, and stewards of the planet. And home is a sanctuary to protect your children so they can learn lessons of caring and contribution at their own developmental pace and with your support, guidance, and respect.

A loving home is free of fear, which is the source of all conflict. It is a place where children trust that their needs matter and that everyone's needs—theirs included—will be considered and cared for. They can then relax into the life that calls them forth with such urgency—and find their place in the net of giving and receiving that forms a family, a community, a nation, and a world.

Respectful Parents, Respectful Kids is primarily about parent-child relationships. The processes and suggestions for improving respect and co-operation apply to all ages of children and are also very effective in communicating with adult family members. Each of the three parts of this book will contribute to a parent's growing capacity to create a respectful, loving home.

Part I. The Foundation for Respect & Co-operation

The three chapters of Part I focus on the underlying dynamic that links the two things that parents say they want most: respect and co-operation.

Part II. The 7 Keys to Co-operation

The 7 keys that make up Part II gradually develop parents' capacity to establish a home as a No-Fault Zone—a place where valuing every family member's needs equally and doing one's best to meet them replaces fault-finding, punishment, and reward.

Part III. Family Activities & Stories from the No-Fault Zone

Part III provides a wide range of games, activities, and cut-outs for additional skill development as well as for fun and further exploration. For inspiration and real-life stories from parents who are using the processes introduced in this book, go to the end of Part III for Stories from the No-Fault Zone. (All stories, throughout this book, use fictional names.)

A Note about Nonviolent Communication

While Nonviolent Communication (NVC) is a foundational element of this book, it is presented here as a means or vehicle for arriving at a state of mind and heart that is the deeper goal. Although you will be introduced to the specific language components of NVC in Key 5, the emphasis of this book is not so much on the mechanics of the language as on the inner posture of respectful parenting. The practice of NVC transforms dualistic, adversarial, and fearful thinking—which is the source of internal and external conflict—into a respectful, loving awareness of the life-enriching human needs at the core of all behavior.

PART I

The Foundation for Respect & Co-operation

The three chapters of Part I focus on the underlying dynamic that links the two things parents say they want most—respect and co-operation.

Chapter 1 ▪ Respect & Co-operation: What Parents Want and How to Get It

This chapter establishes co-operation as a two-way street and points out the functional distinction between exercising power over children and engaging in power with them.

Chapter 2 ▪ Self-Respect: Parents Have Needs Too

This chapter emphasizes how important it is for parents to take care of their own undeniable needs.

Chapter 3 ▪ What Takes the Co- Out of Co-operation?

This chapter presents the habits of thought and expression that undermine co-operation.

Chapter 1

Respect & Co-operation: What Parents Want and How to Get It

Respect and *co-operation* are high on the list of what parents tell us they want from their kids. Perhaps you are among the many parents who have an automatic voice alarm that periodically goes off in the midst of an argument and says, *I really want more respect and co-operation from these kids!* Perhaps you are among the many parents who wonder what in the world is going on to prevent you from getting the respect and co-operation you want. After all that you do for your kids, aren't these simple things to ask for? Well, yes—and no. Respect and co-operation are simple because they are basic needs you have. On the other hand, setting up the conditions to get them requires more attention than you might think.

We have found that you can tap into a flow of mutual respect and co-operation if you are willing to do the following:

Remember that your children learn what you are living.

Co-operate with your children.

Value your needs and your children's needs equally.

Look at your assumptions about children.

Develop and practice the 7 keys that are at the core of respectful parenting.

> What would happen if even one generation were raised with respect and without violence?
>
> —Gloria Steinem

Though moms and dads talk a lot about respect and co-operation, we find that confusion surrounding the terms is rampant. When asked, parents aren't quite sure what they mean each time they use the words; they can even mean different things at different times. And, to top it off, the ways parents go about trying to get respect and co-operation often backfire because they haven't been able to show their kids either respect or co-operation—at least in the way this book presents the terms.

Co-operation Is a Two-Way Street

It turns out that many parents, instead of thinking of co-operation as a two-way working relationship with their kids, think of it as a one-way street where kids do what parents want them to do. When kids don't do what is expected, they are called *uncooperative*, and from that point on the situation can easily turn into name-calling, criticizing, blaming, arguing, and fighting. Later attempts to patch things up often resort to compromises, negotiations, and bargaining, which rarely meet anybody's needs fully.

Explore for Yourself

What does the word *co-operate* mean to you?

Have you ever said something to your child like the following? *Your room is a mess; I want you to clean it up before you go to the game.* Have you then wondered why she didn't do what she was told to do, right away and with a smile? You made a unilateral decision, and she was expected to carry it out according to your time frame and standards. Because, *After all, I'm the parent!* This attitude, however, fails to consider the child's point of view. When you neglect to consider your child's thoughts, feelings, needs, and possible solutions to getting the room cleaned, you do so at the risk of losing her respect and goodwill. Your child's grumbling resistance is, in effect, a natural consequence of your choice to operate without her input.

The *co-* in *co-operate* means *together*, as in co-creator, co-author, and co-worker. *Oper* means *to work*, so *co-operate* means *to work together*. True co-operation is not something you can mandate. When there is no *togetherness* in the operation of a home—as in mutual agreement about rules that affect a child's life as well as mutual problem solving and decision making—then you can expect the following natural consequences: resistance, arguments, hurt feelings, battles of will, and reliance on punishments and rewards. A fundamental law of human relations is: No *co-* in the household operations leads to resistance, which leads to punishments and rewards to force compliance, which leads to further resistance, and so forth. Parents who leave out the *co-* in their household operations are destined to reap the consequences of this omission. If you aren't working with your children, they aren't going to want to work with you.

A young woman shared this story with us: Her father used to make her clean her room to very strict specifications; he even lifted up the edge of the carpet in an otherwise clean room and punished her if she had failed to sweep up a few crumbs. The more he insisted that things be done his way, the more she was filled with hostility and resistance. She cleaned her room because she was afraid of her father and feared what would happen if she didn't. It was cleaned with spite rather than the desire to co-operate and contribute to the smooth functioning of the home.

How different might this situation have been if she and her father had agreed upon standards together? If she had been included in deciding whether or not the room was clean?

> Together we can be wiser than any of us can be alone. We need to know how to tap that wisdom.
>
> —Tom Atlee

Explore for Yourself

How might you be leaving out the *co-* in your household operations?

If you are leaving the *co-* out of your operations, what are the consequences of your actions?

List at least one thing you can do to contribute to co-operation in your home.

Co-operation Is a Survival Skill

Co-operation is a goal for parents—something they would like more of, more often. It's also a skill to develop. In order to sustain itself and thrive, every species on the planet has to learn this skill. Our ability as humans to survive and thrive in an increasingly interconnected global society depends more and more upon learning and practicing the fine points of co-operation.

Human beings have been operating in a fiercely competitive mode for over ten thousand years[1]—exerting power over others to gain tribal, national, or personal advantage. Power imbalances and disregard for the basic needs of millions of people, as well as the needs of nonhuman species and the earth itself, have resulted in ongoing conflicts, wars, and devastation. There are many economic, social, and ecological indicators that the way our species has been operating is unsustainable and a new mode of co-operating, or sharing power, is needed. As parents learn to foster co-operation in families, they become models of change for their children, for other parents, and for community members. They also become active participants in creating an evolutionary shift toward global peace and sustainability.

---

1. Eisler, *The Chalice and the Blade*; Sahtouris, *EarthDance*; Wink, *The Powers That Be*.

Co-operation—A Skill for Sustainability

According to evolutionary biologist Elisabet Sahtouris, co-operation is the only way toward sustainability. Mature ecosystems such as prairies and rainforests evolve when there is more co-operation than there is hostile competition. The highly complex ecosystem of the rainforest is a particularly vivid example of a mature system that has survived through millions of years because species learned to co-operate with each other. In the rainforest, "every species is fully employed, all work cooperatively while recycling all of their resources, and all products and services are distributed in such a way that every species remains healthy. *That* is sustainability."[1]

1. Sahtouris, "Skills for the Age of Sustainability," 3.

People who live on family farms and in small communities need no reminder of the necessity for co-operation. Barn raisings, potlucks, and community harvests have been the norm for hundreds of years. However, those of us who live in more isolated family units are apt to forget that we all walk on the ground of interconnectedness. We can forget, that is, as long as things go smoothly—until something happens that affects the whole. When a major employer closes down business in a community, everyone feels the economic, social, and personal impact. In 2004, when a mountain slid down and covered several homes in the small town of La Conchita, California, those of us in neighboring towns felt the impact and got involved, rallying around families who lost homes and loved ones. And one year later when hurricanes Katrina and Rita brought floods that destroyed thousands of lives in New Orleans and other cities and towns in the southern United States, the whole country saw itself as one interconnected net of pain and personal, social, economic, and environmental concerns.

When the flow of community life is interrupted by natural or man-made crises—when survival is clearly at stake—something deep in us is touched, and we are made aware of the ground of interconnectedness that supports us as a community and as a species. This recognition of our interdependence—that we are each a part of a vast web of life, and our well-being is intimately linked to the well-being of others—shows us why co-operation is a skill to develop, not only for harmony at home, but also for our survival as a human family.

Families are core units in our net of interdependence, and the impact of the relationships in your family will be felt for generations to come through the lives of your children and grandchildren. The way that you parent will affect not only your child, but the lives of hundreds and perhaps thousands of people in your child's future. You don't have a choice about whether or not to affect the net of interdependence; however, you do have a choice about *how* you affect it.

Co-operation Is Using Power *With* Your Kids

Consider that at every moment your interactions with your children are based on either exercising power *over* them or exercising power *with* them. You may be quite familiar with both kinds of interactions; very likely, one of these is predominant in your family life. Which is it?

Power-Over Parenting

Expressions of *power-over* parenting:

> *I want you to do this right now. If you don't . . .*
>
> *Don't make me ask you again!*
>
> *You just have to do what you're told.*
>
> *No back talk from you!*
>
> *I don't care what you think about it!*
>
> *I know you want to play but you have to . . .*
>
> *How many times do I have to tell you?*

Building on a power-over foundation means that you determine what is best and right for your children, you give instructions, and you enforce your child's obedience. Parents with this orientation spend a lot of their time lecturing, advising, arguing, analyzing, and, in whatever ways, trying to manage the behavior of their children to fit a set of expectations they accept as the *right* and *only* way to do things. In their efforts to ensure compliance, parents often find themselves commanding and demanding, using phrases like *you have to, you must, you ought to,* and *you should.* They also have to enforce commands with threats of punishment and promises of rewards. Children have no choices or very few choices and are infrequently, if ever, asked for input to solve their own problems.

Power-With Parenting

Expressions of *power-with* parenting:

> *I'd like us to find a solution that works for everyone.*
>
> *I'm happy when we work together.*
>
> *I feel sad when one of us is left out of decisions.*
>
> *I'd like to hear how this sounds to you.*
>
> *I'm wondering what you need right now.*
>
> *Would you be willing to . . .?*
>
> *Please help me understand what you have in mind.*
>
> *I wonder what your thoughts are when you hear that.*

The soul empties itself of all its own contents in order to receive the being it is looking at, just as he is, in all his truth.

—Simone Weil

Building on a power-with foundation means that parents and children co-operate to determine what is best for the children, actions are mutually agreed upon, and family members get together periodically to review agreements they have made. Parents with this orientation use precious parenting time actively listening to their kids and attempting to understand them by hearing their feelings, needs, and wishes. This parent's primary message is, *I want us to come up with strategies and solutions that work for all of us. I'm willing to explore with you until we can do that.* Compromising, negotiating, and bargaining—where someone is usually left dissatisfied—are poor substitutes for getting to the roots of problems and meeting needs to everyone's satisfaction.

Parents determined to exercise power *with* their children are not afraid to listen to what their kids have to say. In fact, they welcome it. They realize that listening to children does not mean they agree or disagree with them. They know that listening is often just the beginning of a dialogue, and, especially if they listen first, they will have opportunities to honestly share their own thoughts, feelings, and needs as well.

Whether you are building on a power-over or a power-with foundation, your children are learning from everything you say and do. Kids pick up the tactics you are using and use them with their siblings and friends. They take these same tactics to school as their foundation for interactions with classmates, and they use them to build a foundation for their future relationships.

Respect Is a Way of Seeing

The good news is that willing co-operation between you and your child is not only possible, it is a natural consequence of a relationship where there is mutual respect. Respect, like co-operation, is often misunderstood and used in a variety of ways.

What do you mean when you say you want more respect from your children? Do you want them to be more willing to listen and learn from you? Do you want more understanding for your own circumstances and needs? Is it fewer arguments you want? Would you like your kids to see that your point of view is right? Do you mean you want admiration and high regard from your children? Or, do you want them to do what you say, no questions asked? Perhaps you mean all of the above. With so many different ways of understanding respect, is it any wonder that it is so difficult to ask for and get it? For most parents *respect* is a catch-all word that implies many thoughts, feelings, and needs.

> Parenting takes place in a dynamic exchange among all members of a family. By living authentically in relation to one another, there is a sense of aliveness and joy that we do not have when we aim to teach, preach, or get others to do what we want.
>
> —Joseph Chilton Pearce

Explore for Yourself

What does the word *respect* mean to you?

The core meaning of the word *respect* is *to look*. But to look at what? We propose that *to respect* another person is to look at what they are experiencing—in particular, to look with respect to their present feelings and needs.

When looking at your child, you can always choose your focus. You can look at their behavior from your point of view, from your desires and your judgments. Or you can look at them from their point of view, with respect to how they are feeling and what they need.

Focusing on Misbehavior

When you focus on what's wrong with a child, it can sound like this: *How could you be so careless? I thought you were more mature than that! What's wrong with you? You know better; you should be ashamed.*

When you focus on what's wrong with what your child did, it can sound like this: *That was a terrible thing to say. Look what you've done! You should know better!*

When your focus is clouded by your fears about what your children will do in the future, it can sound like this: *If you keep that up, you won't ever succeed. You're never going to make friends the way you're acting. When are you going to start listening to me?*

Parenting that focuses on what's wrong with children or what's wrong with their actions relies on a belief that scolding them, making them feel bad, and punishing them will motivate them to act differently. Does it work for you?

Focusing on Needs

No matter how crazy your child's actions may seem to you, from tugging on your pant leg to yelling, hitting you, hitting siblings, or throwing a toy, all that your child is trying to do at that moment is fulfill a need—a need that you have, too. Maybe the need is for attention, consideration, choice, or autonomy. You may not like the way your child is trying to meet his need, but you will have the best chance of connecting with him—and also of helping him find a better way—if you recognize the need he's sincerely trying to meet at that moment.

The dad in the following story was elated to find he could focus on his son's needs rather than react to his behavior. Two months into the start of middle school, twelve-year-old Jason was putting on weight. His parents stocked the house with healthy foods but knew that he was snacking on chips and candy at school and on the weekends. His parents didn't want to put additional pressure on him by saying something, but one night Jason said angrily, *I can't believe I'm so fat!* His dad reports that his first inclination was to lecture Jason: *Look, if you'd just lay off the junk food you'd lose weight.* He was proud of the fact that he kept quiet instead, hoping to hear more from Jason about what was going on with him. Sure enough, Jason continued, *I know it's all the junk I'm eating, but I can't stay away from it. I crave it after school and it's everywhere I go.* Dad empathized with Jason by guessing his feelings and needs: *Sounds like you're feeling kind of stuck right now? You'd like to find another way to let off steam and relax besides eating fatty foods? At the moment you don't know what that could be?* Tears welled up in Jason's eyes as his anger toward himself shifted to sadness. *Yeah, Dad, I've got to do something!* Dad empathized again: *You sound pretty motivated to change some habits.* Jason replied, *I am, Dad. Do you have any ideas?*

Like most parents would, this dad jumped at his son's invitation to share his opinions and discuss ideas about what his son could do to meet his needs in healthier ways.

Co-operation Is In Our Genes

The idea that co-operation is a necessity for life to survive and thrive, and that it is part of our genetic wiring, is put forth by both scientists and spiritual leaders.

A natural instinct among animals to co-operate for mutual well-being has been reported by biologists Tim Roper and Larissa Conradt. In their study *Group Decision-Making in Animals*, they conclude that the natural state of all group-living animals, including humans, is co-operation, not domination. They maintain that Nature has endowed humans with a biofeedback system that includes the release of endorphins, and joyful feelings, when we give to one another.[1] These feelings motivate us to continue to give, and thereby to contribute to the survival of the species and more: the thriving or all-around well-being of each of us.

Tenzin Gyatso, the Dalai Lama, also claims that co-operation is a natural response in humans because we are social creatures, and our survival and well-being is inextricably linked with the well-being of others. The impulse to give to others and to co-operate with them for mutual well-being is, thus, grounded in our nature. In his words, "interdependence is a fundamental law of nature. Not only higher forms of life but also many of the smallest insects are social beings who, without any religion, law, or education, survive by mutual cooperation based on an innate recognition of their interconnectedness."[2]

A working definition of co-operation that emerges from these perspectives is this: *Co-operation is a way of engaging in power with others for mutual well-being.*

---

1. Roper and Conradt, "Group Decision-Making in Animals."
2. Gyatso, "Compassion and the Individual," http://www.john-bauer.com/dalai-lama .htm (accessed January 17, 2006).

Chapter 2

Self-Respect:
Parents Have Needs Too

Parents are born into parenting with the arrival of their first child. Unlike in past generations, when extended families provided a network of connections among different age groups, for many of us the arrival of our first child is our first experience of being with a newborn, let alone caring for one 24/7. And it quickly dawns on us that we are on our own, with neither job training nor so much as an instruction manual or a CD like the one that came with our cell phone, for this—the most challenging and important job of our lives! It is sobering to realize that a want ad for a job as a parent would read *No training or previous experience required.*

And so, at your birth into parenting you were irrevocably thrust into a wildly new dimension of life, equipped primarily with your biological drive to survive, your natural inquisitiveness, and a vast innate capacity to learn and grow—just like your newborn baby. It can be a humbling experience to see how little you know and how much there is to learn about living with children. The fact is, you are learning about family relationships, co-operating, and caring, right along with your kids. On especially challenging days, your life experience and advanced capacity for reasoning and problem solving may not seem to count for very much.

The learning curve for parenting is steep; it often becomes steeper as children get older, and you might despair at ever getting ahead of it. In the face of this all-day–every-day job that lasts for approximately eighteen years and has such important implications for a child's future, many parents become consumed by what their kids need and forget to take

> When we begin to know ourselves in an open and self-supportive way, we take the first step in the process that encourages our children to know themselves.
>
> —Daniel J. Siegel

care of themselves. Some parents believe that being a good parent means they should sacrifice their own needs, entirely. A father of six stood up in the middle of one of our parenting workshops to say, *It's ridiculous to talk about parents' needs. You just have to face the fact that when you parent, you have to sacrifice your needs for eighteen years.* This father sounded grim and resolved, and we felt sad for him and his children. Giving to your children while sacrificing your own needs comes at a high cost to everyone.

Your Needs Matter!

The bottom-line reality—that your needs matter and that you must first care for yourself before others—is demonstrated by the airlines when they direct parents, in case of emergency, to first place the oxygen mask on themselves, and then place a mask on their child. It is easy to see, in this case, that parents will be of no use to their children if they themselves can't breathe.

Parenting off the plane is no different, just less obvious. In either case, meeting your needs is nonnegotiable. If you are not taking care of your needs so that you are thriving, you may be able to help your children survive, but you will not have the vitality and presence you need to help them thrive. Nor will you be modeling what it takes to care for oneself, which is what your child will need more than anything when she moves out on her own.

Parents' needs do matter, and they require more attention and resources than most communities presently offer. We dream of having a place in every community where parents can go on a regular basis to recharge their batteries, learn, and create community. We can easily imagine school campuses transformed into community centers that serve families during evening hours and on weekends. While children are busy with activities, parents could receive empathy, coaching, and the companionship of other parents. They could also do yoga, tai chi, group singing, cooking classes, or get a massage. Parents and other community members could gather more often to address critical social and

What we are teaches the child far more than what we say, so we must be what we want our children to become.

—Joseph Chilton Pearce

economic needs in their community. We like to imagine a world that includes lots of support like this for parents and families.

This book is not a substitute for the family and parent support we'd like to see in the world, but we hope it will inspire you to identify and value your needs, as well as the needs of your children. We live in hectic times; it's difficult, if not impossible, to take good care of all of your needs all of the time. The intention to do your best in this regard is a big step forward.

Meet Your Need to Know What You Need

Most of the parents we meet aren't doing a great job of taking care of their needs because they don't know what their needs are. Like most parents, you were probably raised to give up your needs in order to live up to external standards and expectations determined by your parents, teachers, and employers. Giving up needs was and still is the norm in all structures where people use power over others—including families, schools, and governments. It has been shocking and sad for us to realize how readily parents and teachers, throughout history, have subdued the passionate urgencies of infants and young children in favor of obedience and conformity.

After years of having overlooked needs, many adults tell us they feel numb; they want to feel more impassioned, alive, and free, the way they felt in early childhood. Many have erased early memories and given up on or are suspicious of any mention of feelings or needs—referring to people who talk about them as *touchy-feely*, *soft*, or *needy*. Yet parents we work with who learn to reconnect with their feelings and needs experience a renewed sense of vitality and aliveness. They also become more effective at providing for their needs.

Recognize the Cost of Not Meeting Your Needs

When your days are full, fast, and frenzied and you aren't getting rest, regular meals, or time to relax, it's difficult to respond enthusiastically or well to the needs of your kids. When you are not making time for fun in your life, you are apt to be less than thrilled by your children's insistence on having so much of it. When you don't have someone to listen to you, you might feel overwhelmed with the challenges of listening to your kids.

The emotional costs of letting your energy tanks drain dry, and running on empty, are felt not only by you but by your kids as well. You will find yourself in lose/lose interactions with your kids—nagging, threatening, yelling, making demands, and doling out rewards and punishments. Eventually you will come to a sputtering stop—the point of exhaustion and overwhelm where you just burn out. Full of self-doubt, helplessness, and hopelessness, you are likely to question the meaning and purpose of what you're doing, say things you never meant to say, and threaten things you don't really want to happen.

Another effect of allowing your needs to go unmet for long periods of time is that you are apt to become resentful. When your children realize the price you are paying to care for them, they may feel guilty about receiving from you and resist or even refuse what you offer. At the same time, they are likely to get the mistaken impression that you are someone who doesn't have needs. And if they aren't aware of what your needs are, they won't be able to contribute to fulfilling them. One way or another, your ability to give joyfully to your children and the joy they could have in giving to you will be compromised.

Kids are empathic by nature and want and need to see themselves as givers. (Of course, there are limits to what they can contribute toward meeting the needs of parents, and they can't be expected to be a primary source for parents' needs.) A friend related this story about how her child found a way to help when he knew what was needed:

One afternoon my two-year-old son and I had been playing together for quite a long time, and I was feeling very tired. I wanted to take a short nap, but he was still energetic and wanted to continue to play. I told him I was tired and needed a rest. He kept insisting that I play with him. Finally, I shifted to his point of view and said, *I hear that you are having a lot of fun playing with me and that you don't want to stop; you just want to keep playing.* I was so tired I couldn't think of much more to say. I think he caught on to the intent of what I was trying to say because something shifted for him. It wasn't long before he came up with his own strategy. He said: *Mummy, you lie down, and I will lie down next to you.* And, that's what we did. He entertained himself and allowed me to nap for a half hour. When I got up he asked me, *Mummy, have you slept enough?* I was very touched.

Learn New Habits to Take Care of You

There is much to be said for learning, before a crisis occurs, to recognize the warning signs that you aren't taking care of yourself. It takes a great deal of commitment and persistence to set aside old habits of self-denial and self-sacrifice and develop new habits of self-acceptance and self-respect. However, we have seen many parents do just that when they recognized how not taking care of themselves was contributing to family stress and conflict. Before you find yourself once again running on empty, try to (1) notice the warning signs that you are run down or about to say or do something you will regret, (2) pause and take a few deep breaths, and (3) take *Time In*, to connect with yourself. (See "Take *Time In*" in Part III, Topic: Life-Enriching Practices.)

Exercise: Take 10

If you are a parent who is neglecting the basic requirements for your well-being, you can break the cycle of self-sacrifice by taking just ten minutes a day for yourself. These few minutes are a big improvement over taking no time at all. You can use this time to reflect on what's important to you, to remember what you are grateful for, to meditate or pray, to read something inspiring, to appreciate yourself for your efforts, to give yourself empathy for your challenges, or to celebrate how you are meeting your needs.

> If there is anything that we wish to change in our children, we should first examine it and see whether it is not something that could better be changed in ourselves.
>
> —Carl G. Jung

Exercise: Find Out What You Need

We invite you to read over the following list of needs—needs we all have. Parents we work with have found value in using this list to reflect on the needs they are meeting and those they'd like to meet better. Some people just take mental note as they scan the list; others put a plus sign by needs they are meeting and a minus sign next to needs they are not meeting and would like to. Parents report that this exercise, done periodically, helps them stay current with themselves. They also tell us that when they are aware of needs they want to meet, simple ways to meet them more readily appear.

Parents (and all people) need:

Rest	Companionship
Exercise	Honesty
Healthy Food	Empathy
Learning & Growth	Support
Fun	Meaning
Creativity	Contribution
Purpose	

(For more examples of needs, see "Needs List" in Part III, Topic: Family Meetings.)

Meet Your Need for Healing Past Pain

A major challenge to respectful parenting is the distress you carry from your past, especially the painful experiences you had with your parents when you were growing up. You probably aren't even aware you have this pain until something your child does triggers an unusually intense, automatic reaction.

Your child says *No* and pushes your hands away when you try to buckle his seat belt. You shove the seat belt into place and say, in a gruff voice, *Don't you talk back to me like that!* You start up the car but you're shaking with feelings of guilt and shock. Later on you feel dismayed and wonder, *Where did that come from?* Even later you recognize the voice: *That sounds just like my mother! I never thought I'd say that!*

Urgent, automatic reactions—when they are not in response to a true emergency—are indicators that you are experiencing what Daniel Goleman calls an "emotional hijacking."[1] At these times, your neocortex—the part of your brain where reasoning takes place—shuts down to allow the primitive brain in charge of survival to take over. When this happens, you have three choices: fight, flee, or freeze. At these moments it's easy to think of your child as the problem. Or you might be beyond thinking and just see red and react. Automatic triggers that go off when children push your buttons are like red lights flashing on the dashboard. They are telling you to pull over to the side of the road, stop the engine, and look inside to see what the problem is. Yet your first reaction may be to put your foot on the accelerator, full speed ahead.

Know When to Hit the Pause Button

Since you can't rely on clear, rational thinking when you're in the midst of an intense, automatic reaction, simply notice what the signs are trying to tell you: it could be an unmet need of yours that is shouting for attention, or pain from your past that is being restimulated. In both cases, push the pause button before you react, and take a *Time In*.

Know When to Ask for Help

When pain from your past comes up frequently, take action outside the family as soon as possible. Healing pain from the past takes time and can best be facilitated by good friends, counselors, or therapists. If you are willing to make the journey, it can be an exciting time of reconnection with yourself that will allow you to bring more clarity, understanding, and harmony to family interactions.

---

1. Goleman, *Emotional Intelligence*.

Meet Your Need for Support and Inspiration

We hope you will find many ways to keep your energy tanks full, beginning with making sure you get rest, regular meals, and recreation. We hope you will also get in the habit of taking short, daily inspiration breaks to remind you of your intentions for parenting; you can read a paragraph in this book, reflect on a quotation, or review one of the charts. We expect that, as you develop greater awareness of your needs, you will begin to notice them more often and sooner and take care of them more reliably and effectively. You can be that vital, alive person you want to be, for your own well-being and that of your children.

Your Self-Regard Matters

There is nothing like parenting to show you your shortcomings and less-than-perfect places. There is no one like your own child to test your relationship ability and agility in the moment, over and over and over again. And to let you know when your walk does not match your talk. With so many mirrors held up to your humanness, there is the possibility for great learning. However, much depends on what you do when you see your less-than-compassionate thoughts and your less-than-perfect actions. Will you judge and berate and punish yourself? Or will you observe your imperfections with compassion, take stumbles in stride, and learn from mistakes while keeping self-respect?

Since there is always something new to learn—about yourself, about your kids, about your relationships—you can't expect a perfect performance. In fact, any thoughts about being a perfect parent or a good parent will add an extra degree of difficulty. If, instead, you will approach parenting practice as seriously and reverentially as professional golfers approach practicing golf swings, or professional musicians approach practicing their instruments, you will avoid the huge handicap of entertaining self-demanding, self-criticizing thoughts. You will want to have all of your energy and attention available for the task at hand: taking good care of your own needs and caring for the needs of your children.

> Instead of punishing our children by sending them into isolation, let's offer ourselves time-out to discover our own needs, our own true selves. You cannot give to your child until you give to yourself.
>
> —Cheri Huber

Learn from Mistakes with Compassion

The way you handle things you wish you had done differently is powerful modeling for your kids. Compassionate ways to learn from mistakes are specifically addressed in Key 6. These practices begin with an understanding that you are always doing the best you can to meet your human needs. It is not out of evil or ill-intent that you might lash out at your spouse or yell at your child. Beneath each action, as beneath every action a child takes, are human needs—whether you are conscious of them or not. Reminding yourself of this will steer you away from self-judgment and toward self-empathy instead, providing you with positive energy and motivation to practice new habits.

Chapter 3

What Takes the
Co- Out of Co-operation?

In this chapter we invite you to take a closer look at what keeps conflict going and may be getting in the way of co-operation flowing in your home: limited time to connect, labels and comparisons, rewards and punishments, and unproductive ways to communicate. For each of these habits that fuel conflict, we suggest effective alternatives to help you eliminate conflict and lay the ground for respect and co-operation.

A word of caution as you read this chapter: Focusing on sources of conflict may stir up feelings of sadness, disappointment, or discouragement. We hope you will have patience and understanding for the learning process you are going through. If you read this book and do the exercises with a focus on the future and on what you want to create (rather than dwelling on the past and what hasn't worked well) you will be able to learn faster and more joyfully.

> If a child is to keep his inborn sense of wonder, he needs the companionship of at least one adult who can share . . .
>
> —Rachel Carson

Limited Time to Connect

There is much about the daily life of today's parent that can fuel conflict and get in the way of co-operating with kids. Chronically overfull schedules and hurried days add an extra load to parents' already difficult job. However, there is absolutely no way around the necessity to make and take time on a regular basis to connect with your kids—to just hang out together.

Many parents tell us they spend a lot of time with their kids. However, when they take a closer look, they realize that most of that time is spent getting them ready for school or some other event, driving them to soccer practice or any number of other places kids want to be and parents feel obliged to take them, or trying to get them to do things they are *supposed* to do. Keeping older kids active in school and social life involves parents in homework, hobbies, computer games, television, and many other activities. Parents find themselves facilitating their children's lives and often feel sad that there seems to be little time to talk about the things that matter most or to just have fun together.

A CEO of a successful company said, *I wish I had spent more time with my kids when they were younger, especially ages nine to thirteen. I did spend time with them doing things but I wish I had spent much more time just listening to them and talking with them. I thought I'd have a lot more opportunity to do this, but once they became teenagers, they were caught up with their peers and were not as open to me. I now tell my employees with young children to do whatever they need to do to spend lots of time with their young children.*

What You Can Do: *Find Time to Connect*

While your children are still young, get in the habit of simply enjoying each other through playing games, singing, dancing, drawing, taking walks, talking about hopes and dreams, laughing, and snuggling together. Dedicate time each week to being a family. Weekly family meetings are a tried and true way to nurture a lifeline of connection. They are a great way to practice co-operation. A combination of fun activities and time to talk about what's up for everyone and how family life is working provides a balance that all family members can enjoy. These meetings need to be scheduled and prioritized or they won't happen. (For a variety of activities to enjoy with your family, see Part III, Topic: Family Meetings.)

> Not causing harm requires staying awake. Part of being awake is slowing down enough to notice what we say and do.
>
> —Pema Chodron

Labels, Comparisons, and Fault-Finding

Labels are for boxes and files. They work to categorize nonliving things but they don't accurately describe or tell the truth about the alive, changing nature of moms, dads, and kids. Unfortunately, most of us grew up learning to label people. We say, without thinking, *She is so nosy. He is obnoxious. She was very inappropriate. You're rude. I'm too sensitive.* Infants are routinely characterized by parents and relatives as *good* when they are asleep or not bothering anyone and as *bad* when they are upset. By the time we are toddlers, we know that when parents say *Be good!* they usually mean *Be quiet and do what you're told. Don't do anything to bother anyone!*

Labeling people as if they were a thing rather than a living, growing, changing being becomes so habitual that you might not notice when you or others are doing it. If you sit at a mall for an hour listening to conversations, or tune into most any television show, you will hear how often people summarize the behavior of other people and categorize them by using labels.

As well as being inaccurate and hurtful, labels can lead to self-fulfilling prophecies.

If you repeatedly call your child lazy because she hasn't done her chores the way you wanted them done, your child can come to believe she is lazy and to act accordingly. *Why bother trying? Since that is how I'm seen, that's probably how I am.*

The child is also learning to give others (in this case, parents) the power to tell them what they are. They will likely transfer this power to their peers and to our ever-present advertising industry, which thrives on people giving it power to tell them they are deficient in some way and need products to make them something more than they are. Looking outside oneself for validation and identity undermines a sense of self-worth and self-confidence in people of all ages.

Any comparisons you make between your child and others deliver an added blow to their self-esteem: *Why can't you share like your brother does? He is so generous. I wish you could live up to your sister's standards at school.*

She is the smartest in her class. Comparisons, rather than turning on a lightbulb of self-recognition and changing children's behavior, actually trigger hostility, jealousy, separation, discouragement, or rebellion because children's needs to be seen, to be respected, and to be accepted just the way they are, are not being met.

What You Can Do: *Express Yourself Honestly Without Evaluation or Fault-Finding*

Instead of labeling your children as good, bad, lazy, industrious, smart, or stupid, share with them clear observations (without labels and evaluations) about what you see them doing and how it affects you. Instead of saying your son is irresponsible, unpack the label and talk about the behaviors you have seen that lead you to want to use the word. Perhaps your son forgets his lunch in the morning, leaves his coat at school, forgets to turn in his homework, and so on. Now you have something to talk about with your son that he can understand.

Instead of calling your daughter uncaring because she isn't feeding the dog every night as you had agreed, you can make an observation: *I appreciate that four out of seven nights last week you fed the dog without any reminders. I feel very happy when everyone is keeping agreements and working together to take care of things around the house.* You can then talk about how you feel when observing that on other nights, you reminded her to feed the dog: *I feel worried realizing that three nights last week you didn't feed the dog until after I reminded you. I would like to feel confident that the dog would be fed every night even if I weren't here to remind you. I wonder if you can think of a way to remember to feed the dog every night?* It may be that reminding your child is actually the best strategy for now; however, exploring possibilities in this respectful way is more likely to engage willing co-operation than calling her uncaring, lazy, or irresponsible would be.

Rewards and Punishments

Rewards and punishments are standard fare in power-over parenting. They are, in fact, necessary measures when your aim is to get kids to do something against their will. Rewards and punishment are the opposite of respect and co-operation and will result in endless power struggles.

The following items demonstrate some of the high costs of both punishment and reward:

They undermine a child's sense of safety and trust.
They encourage children to work for rewards or to avoid punishment
    instead of doing things because they have intrinsic value to them.
They take away a child's pleasure in doing what you ask.
They take away a child's desire to co-operate with you.
They teach children to reward and punish others to get what they want.

Deciding not to use punishment or rewards to coerce your kids to do what you want them to do does not mean that you will permit any kind of behavior or give up on what you need. Respectful interactions mean that each person's needs are valued and taken into consideration with the intent of meeting as many needs as possible.

Punitive vs. Protective Use of Force

There are times when force is needed to protect people or things that you value.

If your child starts to rip up a book, by all means, hold her until she calms down enough to talk together. In this case, force is used for the purpose of protecting something you value, not punishing a wrongdoer. Instead of lecturing her (*You shouldn't hurt books. That's not okay.*) you can empathize first, either out loud or silently (depending on how upset your child is, her age, and what you think would bring the most connection): *Are you feeling frustrated and need to let some energy out? If so, I'd like to help you do this in a way that doesn't hurt you or something I care about, like this book.*

> You can't make your kids do anything. All you can do is make them wish they had. And then, they will make you wish you hadn't made them wish they had.
>
> —Marshall B. Rosenberg

If there is no criticism, blame, or fault-finding in your message, and you remember that every action is an attempt to meet a need, your daughter will be more open to talking about the needs she was trying to meet by ripping the book. Knowing her need, you can then co-operate to discuss other strategies that would fulfill her needs without hurting anything.

This kind of conversation that everyone learns from cannot happen as long as your goal is to inflict pain for a wrong your daughter has committed. If she thinks she is going to be punished, she is likely to shut down or lash out in fear, anger, resentment, and discouragement. Her thoughts are more likely to be about how to get even with you rather than about what she can do differently in the future. And, if you are focused on punishment, you may never get to the reason why she did this in the first place and she may continue to rip things up in the future. Wouldn't you prefer that your daughter stop her behavior because she knows people will listen to her when she wants to speak rather than because she is afraid of what will happen to her if she destroys things?

What You Can Do: *Be Clear about What You Want from Your Kids*

When you want something from your kids, ask yourself the following two questions:

What do I want my child to do?

What do I want my child's reasons to be for doing what I want them to do—guilt, shame, fear of punishment, to get a reward, or to participate and to contribute to their well-being and the well-being of the family?

Notice: When children do something because they feel guilty, ashamed, afraid of punishment, or anxious to get a reward, you will pay a big price. Guilt, shame, and punishment often trigger anger and revenge. Rewards trigger behaviors very much like addiction: you will be required to continually offer bigger rewards to get the compliance you want.

Decide: Is it worth it to you to interact with your children in ways that trigger their guilt, shame, anger, revenge, and bargaining for bigger rewards?

> Where did we ever get the crazy idea that in order to make children do better, first we have to make them feel worse?
>
> —Jane Nelsen

Habits of Thinking and Communicating

Even when your objective is to connect respectfully with your kids, habitual ways of listening and talking to them can get in the way. Throughout this book we will distinguish between communication that fuels conflict and communication that defuses conflict and facilitates co-operation.

The use of two words—in particular, the words *but* and *should*—dramatically affect how your kids will respond to what you say. Notice how often you use these two words and the responses you receive from your kids when you use them.

Imagine you are your child hearing the following messages: *I really had fun with you at the game, but . . . I know you're having fun playing, but . . . I hear what you're saying, but . . .* Kids know exactly what is coming next—something that should be done differently. And that's the only part of your statement that they will hear and register. The word *but* is an eraser: it wipes out everything that was said before it.

The word *should* is even more dangerous. When you use the word *should*—and any of its forms including *must, need to,* and *ought to*—you are actually saying *I know what's best for you, and without checking in with you to see what you think and feel about it, I'm going to tell you what to do.* There is nothing that triggers a child's distress faster than a parent's demands. When your kids hear demands or commands, fear and anxiety are stimulated, the reasoning centers of the brain shut down, and they go into fight, flight, or freeze mode. You have no doubt experienced them digging in their heels, tuning you out, or otherwise shutting down.

The word *should* also communicates to kids that you have an ideal or expectation of what they *should* be. If you are holding on to ideals or expectations about how your child should be, you are likely to miss what your child is trying to express. And their deep needs to be seen and heard, to be accepted, and to feel safe will go unmet.

The degree to which you entertain *should* thinking will also determine the amount of anger you experience. It is should thinking—not what other people do—that is the cause of anger and other negative

It is an open question whether any behavior based on fear of eternal punishment can be regarded as ethical or should be regarded as merely cowardly.

—Margaret Mead

feelings and emotions. When what you are seeing and hearing doesn't match how you think things should be, the difference between the ideal and the real trigger your emotions. Should thinking then lashes out to blame, criticize, and shame others. (Alternately, blame, criticism, and shame can be directed towards yourself, in which case you will feel depressed.) The same should thinking that provokes anger, conflict, and aggression between parents and children is also what contributes to pain and aggression between groups, political parties, and nations throughout the world. (For more about should thinking, see "Transform Anger" in Part III, Topic: Life-Enriching Practices.)

What You Can Do: *Use a Language of Respect*

Additional communication tools that facilitate respectful connection and co-operation are found throughout this book. They are most specifically addressed and explored in Key 5.

Summary

We hope the three chapters that make up Part I leave you with helpful insights, inspiration, and encouragement to continue growing in parenting. These are the main points we'd like to leave with you here: (1) children learn from who you are and what you do rather than what you tell and teach them, (2) children will usually respond in kind when respect and co-operation are shown to them, (3) your needs and your children's needs are equally important, and (4) you can replace habits that fuel conflict with those that defuse and resolve conflict.

With this ground and basic structure in place, we now move on to the 7 keys to respectful parenting. In these keys we show you how to work with kids to turn conflict into co-operation and unlock the door to the kind of home parents and kids can enjoy living in together.

PART II

The 7 Keys to Co-operation

The 7 keys that make up Part II gradually develop parents' capacity to establish a home as a No-Fault Zone—a place where valuing every family member's needs equally and doing one's best to meet them replaces fault-finding, punishment, and reward.

Key 1 ▪ **Parent with Purpose** helps you align with your deepest reasons for parenting and your deepest desires for your children.

Key 2 ▪ **See the Needs Behind Every Action** takes the mystery out of why children act the way they do and introduces a needs-focused approach to parenting.

Key 3 ▪ **Create Safety, Trust, & Belonging** draws upon scientific research to confirm the crucial role that physical and emotional safety plays in children's development, and then shows you how to provide it.

Key 4 ▪ **Inspire Giving** invites you to identify your child's gifts, receive them gratefully, and encourage a mutual flow of giving and receiving.

Key 5 ▪ **Use a Language of Respect** walks you, step by step, through the process language of Nonviolent Communication, showing how you can translate all criticism and blame into respectful expression of needs.

Key 6 ▪ **Learn Together As You Go** encourages you to explore, investigate, and co-create with your children, with the confidence that there are many ways to do things and many strategies to meet needs.

Key 7 ▪ **Make Your Home a No-Fault Zone** reveals the true source of conflict and the path you can take to transform conflict situations into heartfelt connections.

Key 1 ▪ Parent with Purpose

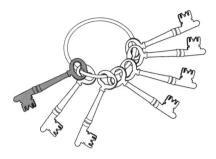

Key Concepts

- Choose your purpose.
- Choose to think in alignment with your purpose.
- Choose to act in alignment with your purpose.
- Choose to listen and talk in alignment with your purpose.
- Choose to encourage your kids' choices.

Three vital questions for parents:

What is important to you?

What are you parenting for?

What is your intention in interacting with your kids?

As the speed of life accelerates, everyone needs something solid to hang on to—some ballast for the high seas and a compass to navigate the dizzying array of choices you face every day. You need to know what purpose you are serving, what you are choosing *for*.

Your children also need to navigate through their own galaxy of choices, fueled by fads, ads, and ever-changing *must have*s. They also need a calm home port to anchor in when their lives are rough-and-tumble.

Parents who are able to define meaning and purpose for their lives, including their parenting lives, help meet vital needs for children, including stability, security, safety, and guidance in how to find one's own pole stars.

> **You must be the change you want to see in the world.**
>
> —Gandhi

▪ Choose Your Purpose

Pressures to work harder, achieve more, and have more are at an all-time high. Moms, dads, and kids, too, are speeding up to keep up, which means operating more of the time on autopilot and reacting quickly to circumstances, in a kind of crisis mode. Crisis mode is essential when there is real danger—during a wildfire, a flood, or an accident. In these times of peril, the body delivers adrenaline to make you alert and responsive. Your safety and your life depend on these automatic reactions.

In the past, crises occurred from time to time. Today, however, the pace of life, high performance standards, news media, and instant communication systems combine to create a heightened sense of crisis in daily life, not only for parents, but for kids as well. In short, families are suffering from crisis overload. Stressed parents in a rush snap at kids—and kids snap back (or they dig in their heels and hide out in their rooms). When you and your kids are in crisis overload, family life can become a battle zone characterized by mutual blame and perpetual arguments.

> Responsibility is fostered by allowing children a voice and wherever indicated a choice in matters that affect them.
>
> —Haim Ginott

If you are operating on autopilot, you will probably feel like a victim of circumstances doing your utmost just to get through the day and all the while using habitual ways of thinking, listening, and speaking that add fuel to crises and conflict. When you are in crisis mode, it can be hard to recognize that at every moment you have choices about how to respond.

Nonetheless, from morning to night each of us is continually making choices about how to act, how to talk, and how to listen. Equally important, those who study our inner lives have gathered strong evidence that we also actively choose how we think.[1] This is why it is crucial for each of us to know what we are choosing *for*. When we know what we are choosing for and we become aware of the choices we are making, each of us increases our ability to respond to life in ways that support our choices. Clearly knowing what you are parenting for provides you guidance for making daily choices about how to parent.

---

1. Carlson, *You Can Be Happy No Matter What*; Krishnamurti, *Freedom from the Known.*

Clarify Your Purpose

The first, all-important step for each of us is to determine what we want and what we're parenting for. The following three exercises are offered to help you clarify your purpose for parenting. Please take your time with the exercises and see what you discover about yourself.

Exercise 1: What do you want for the long term?

Focusing on the long term puts present actions into perspective and often brings what is most important to you into sharper focus. Two questions can help you get clear what you are parenting for.

Two Guiding Questions:

What qualities do I want to see in my children when they are adults?

1._____

2._____

3._____

4._____

5._____

6._____

7._____

What kind of relationship do I want to have with my children, not only now but in the long term?

What do I notice when I sit with these questions and my answers?

Exercise 2: What will you do?

Please review the qualities you listed in Exercise 1 that you want to see in your adult children. Now apply your list to yourself and you will see more clearly exactly which traits you want to be modeling for your children now.

For every quality you listed as something you value and want to see in your adult children, turn it around to reflect the quality or values you want to live. For example, if you said that you want your adult children to be honest, turn it around and say *I value honesty; I want to tell the truth*. If you want your children to care about their health, say *I value health; I want to care about my health*. These statements can be touchstones to remind you of your purpose and your practice.

Statements of Value	Statements of Intention
1. I value _____ .	I want to _____ .
2. I value _____ .	I want to _____ .
3. I value _____ .	I want to _____ .
4. I value _____ .	I want to _____ .
5. I value _____ .	I want to _____ .
6. I value _____ .	I want to _____ .
7. I value _____ .	I want to _____ .

Next, let your statements of values and intentions lead you to more specific actions you can take to support each value.

Specific Actions I Want to Take

1._____

2._____

3._____

4._____

5._____

6._____

7._____

Explore Together: *Choose Your Purpose*

Exercises 1 and 2, above, can be used for children eight years of age or older to help them find their own purpose. Younger children, or anyone in the family who prefers, can make collages or drawings to show how they see themselves in the future, what is important to them, and what actions they can take to live from their values.

When all members of the family have finished these activities, share them at a family meeting.

Option: You can compile each family member's purpose into one family collage, mission statement, poem, or other creative format. (See Part III, Topic: Family Meetings, for more activities you can enjoy with your family.)

Exercise 3: What is working?

No doubt you are already taking actions that serve your intentions. The following exercise is to draw your attention to what you are already doing that works to support your intention and create the results you want. Acknowledging and celebrating what works is one of the powerful, life-enriching practices parents can use to contribute to their own clarity, self-support, confidence, and balanced perspective.

What am I doing now that supports my values and intentions?

1._____

2._____

> When thinking and thought become more and more automatic, perception becomes less and less adapted to the particular situation.
>
> —David Bohm

3._____

4._____

5._____

6._____

7._____

▪ Choose to Think in Alignment with Your Purpose

Our thought processes determine what we see, what we experience, and how we act. They filter and frame our interaction with the world and everything in it, including ourselves and our loved ones. You might wonder, how do I choose my thoughts? Don't they just happen?

> The secret of life is three words: change through relationship.
>
> —J. Krishnamurti

Thoughts arise, and moment by moment you choose which you invite in and entertain. You are the editor of your thoughts, and you can learn how to direct them to support your parenting purpose.

Anyone who chooses to focus on thoughts of who's right and who's wrong, what's fair and what's unfair, who's bad and who's good, will inevitably spend essential time and energy analyzing, judging, blaming, and criticizing. When you give your energy to analyzing, judging, blaming, and criticizing, you are in a sense voting for conflict. The consequence is that by assuming a conflict-ready stance, you distract your own attention from understanding and meeting the needs that your children are expressing through their behavior.

If you entertain thoughts that people are doing things to you—for example, that your child (or anyone else) is *manipulating* you, *taking advantage of* you, *ignoring* you, or *disrespecting* you—you will often feel annoyed, irritated, and angry. However, when instead you think in terms of the needs that you and your child are trying to meet in every action taken, then you are more likely to feel compassion and connection. And you are much more likely to take action that contributes to your child's well-being as well as your own.

Your thoughts about your children determine how you see them and how you treat them. If you see your children as untrustworthy, you will tend to limit opportunities for them to make decisions and learn about trust. Also, when you say to your children, *I can't trust you*, they are likely to take that message to heart. (See the text box on this page.) If instead you see your children as capable of handling life, you will convey your confidence, treat them with respect, and give them lots of opportunities to make decisions for themselves. Imagine the best for your children; give them the gift of your confidence.

Environment Is More Important than Genes

The new field of epigenetics studies how environmental signals affect and even control the activity of genes. It claims that the operations of the cell are primarily affected by and molded by the cell's interaction with the environment, rather than by its genetic code. The environment of a child—made up of family interactions and the behaviors, beliefs, and attitudes of parents—directly affects the child's subconscious mind and behavior, perhaps throughout their lifetime. This is because children's subconscious is very suggestive to what parents say—and the subconscious takes in all information as fact. When parents make comments to children, like *you're lazy* or *you're mean*, these comments are downloaded into the subconscious memory as the truth and then shape the behavior and potential of the child throughout their life, unless an effort is made to reprogram them.[1]

1. Lipton, *The Biology of Belief*.

▪ Choose to Act in Alignment with Your Purpose

Kids will learn the most from what they see you do. Your ability to take action in alignment with your purpose, action that will take you where you want to go, will teach them the most about how to make good choices that take them where *they* most want to go.

A critical action for parents in these high-stress times is to recognize there are limited hours in the day, days in the week, weeks in the year, and that one cannot do everything. Many parents are overbooked with their own activities and commitments, and then there are the school and social requirements and activities for their kids. This centrifugal force propels kids into little satellite worlds of their own, with their own momentum, concerns, and increasing consumer choices.

If family time together is important to you, every commitment you're tempted to make outside the home needs to be looked at to determine whether it contributes to you getting this hard-to-come-by time. If it doesn't, don't commit. Make the tough choices to keep family life alive when kids are young. Use your creativity to keep it interactive, fun, and meaningful, and your kids are likely to look forward to it too.

Explore for Yourself

Based on your parenting purpose, answer the following two questions:

What activities are central to your purpose?

What activities are not?

▪ Choose to Listen and Talk in Alignment with Your Purpose

The way you listen determines whether any interaction you're having will turn into an exploration and discussion or a disagreement or fight. When you listen to your kids, what are you listening for? Are you listening for errors, missteps, and mistakes, or information that can clarify and help you better understand your kids and their challenges? Are you an open and receptive listener, or are you inclined to take things personally and become defensive? Are your triggers cocked and ready to fire if you hear certain ideas that aren't pleasant to you, or can you hear ideas different from your own with respect and curiosity? Does listening mean being silent until it is your turn to talk, or does it mean an active, silent attempt to hear how things look from another person's point of view?

You have choices about how to listen. If you think that you don't, perhaps because you are feeling too sad, hurt, discouraged, anxious, frustrated, or angry, it means that you need to give yourself empathy or find someone to listen to you. Trying to listen to your child when you are full of intense emotions is difficult. Take responsibility for those intense feelings and find someone who can hear you so you are available at a later time to hear your kids. (See Key 5 for more about empathy and self-empathy.)

Habitual ways of speaking often get in the way of establishing respect and co-operation, at home or anywhere else. These familiar ways of communicating contribute to a tremendous amount of pain in the world, including conflicts that arise every day in families.

These are some common characteristics of this way of communicating:

> It labels: *You're mean. She's bossy. He's dumb. I'm lazy.*

> It judges: *I'm right. You're wrong. We're good. They're bad.*

> It blames: *It's her fault. You should have. I'm to blame.*

> It denies choice: *You have to. You can't. I can't. They made me.*

> It makes demands: *If you don't do what I say, you'll be sorry.*

The greatest revolution in our generation is that of human beings, who by changing the inner attitudes of their minds, can change the outer aspects of their lives.

—Marilyn Ferguson

In Key 5 we introduce a different way of using language—a way that focuses on feelings and needs and gives choices other than labeling, judging, blaming, and demanding.

Tell the Truth about Choice

A parent tells her child, *You have to get dressed right now*. Mom keeps up the reminders even while daughter continues to jump on the bed instead of getting dressed. Clearly, the child doesn't *have to* get dressed. More accurately, there will be consequences if she doesn't.

Parents talk about their own lives in the same way: *I have to take Timmy to school. I have to pick up Kelly after work. I have to go to the gym. I have to get to work. I have to cook dinner. I have to go shopping.* How does it feel when you say these things? What messages about life do your children receive when they hear how much you *have to* do? The truth is, you don't have to do any of those things. It's just that there will be consequences for whichever choice you make.

Consider telling yourself and your kids the truth about choice. When you catch yourself thinking or saying, *I should (or have to or must) eat more healthily*, or *get more rest*, or *have more fun*, or *just listen to the kids without reacting*, ask yourself if this is something you want or something you've been conditioned to believe you should want. If you want it, tell yourself the truth about it: *I want to eat more healthily. I choose to get more rest. I'd like to have more fun. I really do want to listen to the kids without reacting*. Notice how you feel when you tell yourself the truth about choice.

Explore for Yourself

To get clear about the choices you have, make a list of *Things I Choose*. Some examples of things to include on this list are: what I wear, what I eat, how I spend my time, who I spend my time with, and how I spend money.

Next, make a list of *Things Others Choose for Me*. Others can include parents, family, employer, community, church, or government. When you have completed this list, take a moment to consider each entry to see whether, in fact, you do have choice in these situations. For instance, if you say that your parents decide how you spend your holidays, consider the choice you have to go along with your parents' ideas or to do something else.

Explore Together: *What Do I Choose?*

Each family member makes his or her own lists of *What I Choose* and *What Others Choose for Me*. Share your lists with each other. Share what you notice about these lists and what feelings come up during this activity.

▪ Choose to Encourage Your Kids' Choices

One of the actions you can choose to ensure more co-operation than conflict in your home is to encourage your kids to make their own choices whenever possible. Their choices and the lessons they learn from them will be the best teachers they have in their lives. Parents overlook needs for choice at great peril—their own and their children's.

Choice is at the core of human experience at any age. This deep longing to choose our own purpose, beliefs, and actions, no matter what age we are, is fought for and defended in every home, particularly by children whose parents overlook their vital need for autonomy. Opportunities to make choices typically increase with age and experience. The total dependence of infants gives way, day by day and with increasing momentum, to a desire to make choices for themselves—choices about what and when they want to eat, explore, and express themselves. The maturing process is about growing the ability to make choices for oneself, and it is crucial for their development that kids at early ages have many opportunities to make choices and to learn from them.

To appreciate what a child experiences when choices are absent, just notice your own responses when someone says to you, *You can't! You must! You have to! Do it because I said so!* or *If you don't do it, you'll be sorry!* Do you want to co-operate? You can bet that your kids have the same reaction to these messages that you do, and probably twice as strong because they haven't had dozens of years to get accustomed to them.

There are several reasons parents think and do for kids rather than give kids choices about how to think and do for themselves. One reason is that they want to see things done in a certain way—neatly, efficiently, and precisely. Another reason is that it takes more time and patience to let kids do things for themselves. Rushed and harried the way most parents are these days, they find it easier and quicker to just take responsibility and do whatever needs to be done.

All this thinking and doing for kids limits their opportunities to make choices and to get things done using their own brain and muscle power and creates resistance and conflict. Without these opportunities, it is difficult for them to see themselves as capable and competent in their world.

One mother we know remembers sharing opinions with her parents and hearing back, *Oh, you don't believe that! You shouldn't think that!* At an early age she learned to keep her opinions to herself, and even as a grown woman she still doubts that anyone will appreciate them. Such limitations on a child's way of seeing the world can have severe consequences in adult life.

Help your kids become aware of the range of choices they have and convey your confidence that they can handle more choice about their lives. To further exercise their choicemaking muscles and to learn what works and what doesn't, invite them to participate in making rules, agreements, and plans that affect them. Let your kids know that they can rely on you to help them make adjustments when needed and that you are willing to learn along with them as they go. (See Key 6 for more about learning along with your kids.)

> What is required for effective change is continuity of sincere effort to release and let go of inefficient thought patterns from the past.
>
> —Doc Childre

When you talk with your children about choice, be aware that many young people, especially adolescents, feel confused, irritated, or angry when they hear adults talk about making choices. Most kids know that parents, teachers, and other adults make most of the important decisions for them, and their choices often seem limited to just two—to comply with the decisions that come down or to rebel against them. Most kids' experience is of living in the midst of a seemingly endless number of rules and expectations that often don't make sense to them and don't honor their desire and ability to make choices for themselves. They might not believe that they have any control over meeting their own needs. They may need a great deal of empathy for the gap between the autonomy they would like to have and the limited number of choices they have been offered by adults in the past.

Summary

Choose to choose. Determining your purpose for parenting is the first step to reduce conflict and create a flow of co-operation at home. From that point on, it is a matter of learning skills and making daily choices about how to think, listen, act, and talk. We hope this key has expanded your awareness of the areas of your parenting life you have choices about. We also hope that you feel inspired to introduce your kids to an ever-widening range of choices—so that they sense themselves as full participants in their lives, and so they will enter adulthood as competent and confident choicemakers.

Daily Practice

Take time daily to reflect on your purpose.

Remember your intention for your interactions with your children.

Notice *should*s and *have to*s and translate them to *things you want* and *choices you make.*

Key 2 ▪ See the Needs Behind Every Action

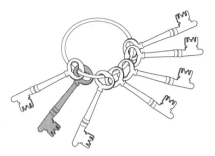

Key Concepts

- All behavior is an attempt to meet a need.
- Children are always doing their best to meet their needs.
- You are responsible for meeting your own needs.
- Feelings are messengers of met and unmet needs.
- Children want to be heard and understood.

Why do we do what we do? Why do our children behave the way they do?

Sometimes, of course, it's easy to understand why people do certain things: Ask a child why he eats, and he'll say he's hungry. Ask why he wants to go out with his friends, he'll say for fun, to play. And why he asks so many questions? Because he wants to know some things. But ask him why he hit his little sister or why he doesn't want to go to school today, and he's not so clear. He's likely to say, *Cuz she's stupid, I hate her,* or *School is dumb!*

Parents often react to statements like these by discounting them: *You don't mean that. That's ridiculous. That's not the problem.* Or they reprimand their child: *You shouldn't talk like that. What a terrible thing to say.* When kids hear this, they will try to defend themselves or they will shut down. And parents will be no closer to understanding what's really going on.

Nor does it help to ask *Who started this?* or *Whose fault was it?* You'll just get more accusations and more strife. This confrontational way of determining who is wrong, who's to blame, and who's deserving of punishment is upheld in homes, in schools, and throughout our justice system. It persists even though it rarely leads to understanding the deeper

> When we understand the needs that motivate our own and others' behavior, we have no enemies.
>
> —Marshall B. Rosenberg

61

motives for actions. Without knowing the deeper motives, you can never really resolve problems or conflicts; you can only put temporary patches on them.

Children, of course, pick up on this approach to conflict and are quick to point the finger of blame: *It's her fault! She started it! She should be punished.* They, understandably, do what they can to protect themselves from blame and punishment. One strategy for this is lying. In fact, we have found that the main reason children (and people of any age) lie is that they don't feel safe telling the truth and they want to protect themselves from being punished. Assigning blame does not solve anything, and when parents assume the roles of judge and jury, determining who is to blame and what's to be done about it, they perpetuate an ongoing blame game at home, where accusations, fault-finding, and name-calling become the norm.

The real voyage of discovery lies not in seeking new landscapes but in having new eyes.

—Marcel Proust

How sad this is, when what every child wants is to be seen for their good intentions and acknowledged for their best efforts. When they are seen with respect, they feel safe. This is especially important when their actions don't turn out so well. When a child feels discouraged, distressed, sad, fearful, or confused about something, it doesn't help to give advice, blame, criticize, shame, or punish. These responses only add to the misery and fear; they don't help kids understand the situation better or learn from their mistakes. When children come to expect these fear-inducing reactions from adults, they decide at some point to find someone else to talk to or they shut down and don't talk at all.

What kids do want, when things go poorly, is someone who listens, accepts their feelings, and recognizes their good reasons for doing what they did. Listening, accepting, and understanding foster self-reflection and learning. When you fulfill your kids' needs for being heard, accepted, and understood, and you allow your kids to reflect on their actions, you send a message that they are competent and resourceful and can learn from every situation. When children receive respectful, empathic listening and feel the relief and hope it brings them, they will come back to talk to you next time. Eventually they will be open to hearing your thoughts and seeking your advice.

■ All Behavior Is an Attempt to Meet a Human Need

Just imagine how you might interact with your child, and with everyone in your life, if at each moment you saw that all of their actions were their best attempts to meet their needs. Human beings share basic survival needs that include air, water, food, rest, and safety. In addition to these basics, we also need love, learning, friends, play, some degree of autonomy, and more. Since people everywhere have these needs in common, it is possible to understand what motivates other people's behavior even when lifestyles, beliefs, languages, and age are different. This understanding increases compassion for others even, and especially, when we disagree with their actions.

For a needs list, see Key 5. You will also find a list of needs at the Center for Nonviolent Communication website (www.cnvc.org). There is no definitive list of human needs; the criteria for any list of needs is that it includes life essentials that are common to every human being, separate from the various strategies people use to meet their needs.

Probably the main reason parents are afraid of listening to what children want is because parents don't understand the difference between a need and a strategy for meeting a need. They are afraid that if they listen to a child's desire for a video game, or a new toy, or to stay up all night, they are setting themselves up either for a fight or for giving in and providing the child with whatever is wanted.

So let's get clear that a new video game is not a need; it is a strategy for meeting needs, which might include the need for relaxation, competency, or fun. Since the main criterion for universal needs is that they are shared by everyone on the planet, and clearly there are people who get along quite well without video games, you can easily determine that video games are not a need. Likewise, talking on the telephone for hours every night or watching cartoons in the morning before school are not needs. Having friends over every day after school is not a need.

Everyday language obscures the distinction between needs and strategies. We say *I need you to eat your broccoli* or *I need you to take a bath right now*. Or we say *I need an iPod*. However, having a child eat broccoli is not a need and neither is buying an iPod. Eating broccoli is a strategy a parent has for meeting the body's needs for nutrition; buying an iPod is a strategy for meeting needs also, for fun, entertainment, relaxation, or belonging. The things that children ask for daily with great urgency and drama are most often strategies for meeting a need.

The reason this distinction between needs and strategies is so important is that practically all conflicts, arguments, fights, and power struggles—with children and everyone else—are fights over strategies and can be resolved, if not prevented, when a parent respectfully focuses on the needs behind the strategy.

A typical strategy-based argument:

Child: *I don't want to go to bed now.*

Parent: *But you have to go to bed now. It's your bedtime.*

Child: *But I'm not tired.*

Parent: *But you will be in the morning if you don't go to bed now.*

Child: *No I won't.*

Parent: *Yes you will.*

Child: *No I won't.*

Arguments like this leave the child frustrated and unheard. The parent is also not being heard for the needs that would be met by having the child go to bed at a particular time. Without understanding and respect for everyone's needs, conflict will likely persist.

If parents first listen respectfully for their child's needs before expressing their own needs, as in the following example, the result is often more connection, understanding, and opportunities to co-operate.

Child: *I don't want to go to bed now.*

Parent: (guessing the child's feelings and needs) *You're having fun playing and want to continue?*

Child: *Yes, and I'm not tired.*

Parent: *So you'd like to go to bed when you're tired?*

Child: *Yes.*

Parent: *Is there anything else?*

Child: *No.*

Parent: *Can I tell you why I'd like you to go to bed now?*

Child: *Okay.*

Parent: *I'd like you to be rested and ready to wake up in the morning for school. I've noticed that when you stay up after nine on school nights, you're tired the next morning. Do you hear the need I have?*

Child: *That I'm rested and want to get up in the morning.*

Parent: *Yes. Thank you for hearing that.*

When both parents and children are heard in this way, there is frequently a shift in energy, an openness to move towards the other, a willingness to find a way to satisfy both of them. The child in this example may be more willing to go to bed soon. Or the parent might be willing to let the child play quietly for a set amount of time before lights go out. A parent's respectful listening does not mean agreement with the child, and it certainly does not mean giving children (or anyone) everything they ask for. If you would like to save yourself endless arguments, battles, and power struggles, learn to differentiate a need from a strategy. (See Keys 5 and 6 for more about needs and strategies.)

> When you make that one effort to feel compassion instead of blame or self-blame, the heart opens again and continues opening.
>
> —Sara Paddison

Explore for Yourself

Wherever you look, you can see people attempting to meet one or more of their needs. We invite you to look at your own life with this respectful perspective and see if it brings new insight.

When you call a friend to talk about something that is troubling you, you usually want to meet needs for understanding and empathy.

When your partner says, at the end of a long day, *I don't want to talk about it or deal with one more thing today!* you can guess they have a need for rest.

When you see your child working on a puzzle with rapt attention, you might guess she is meeting needs for learning, perhaps also for competency, and maybe, too, for relaxation.

When your child tells you a joke, he is probably meeting a need for humor and play, and also, perhaps, for connection with you.

When you ask your two-year-old to put away his toys and he says, *No!* what need do you guess he is trying to meet?

When your twelve-year-old daughter says she has to have the latest style of clothes, what need is she trying to meet?

▪ Children Are Always Doing Their Best to Meet Their Needs

Every moment of every day, your children are doing their best to meet their needs—the same needs that you have. With this understanding of behavior, habits of judging kids' actions will naturally give way to respectful understanding and compassion.

You are also, at each moment, doing the best you can to meet your needs. With this understanding of your behavior, self-judgment can give way to self-respect and compassion. When you focus your attention on your needs, you are able to communicate about what is at the heart of your concerns. You will connect more easily with others, since needs are the same for everyone at any age.

Human beings are wired for well-being through a system of continual needs-messaging. At times needs will announce themselves loudly: *I need food!* At other times they whisper in the background, *I feel confused: I don't even know what I need. I guess that means I need more clarity.* Life delivers these messages so you can be alert to what you need and find skillful ways to fulfill your needs.

▪ You Are Responsible for Meeting Your Own Needs

While you can ask others if they are willing to help you, *you are the only one responsible for meeting your needs.* This can be sobering news. It is also empowering, because it means you are never dependent upon any one person to meet your needs. It is helpful to be clear about this because thinking that another person or a group of people are responsible for your needs has at least two unfortunate outcomes. The first is that you can waste a lot of time waiting for certain others to do things for you when you could be busy finding your own solutions.

The other unfortunate outcome of expecting others to fulfill your needs is that whenever you think in these terms—that others *should, have to,* or *must* do something for you—people will most often hear a demand, which makes giving to you less likely. Demands provoke power struggles and are a major obstacle to joyful giving and willing co-operation.

> Nothing in life is to be feared. It is only to be understood.
>
> —Marie Curie

Explore Together: *What Do People Need?*

What do people need? Why do you do the things you do?

During a family meeting, ask your family if they will explore these questions with you. There is no definitive list of universal needs, and yours may vary from another person's to some degree. However, these lists will have more similarities than differences if everyone applies the litmus test of needs: *Is it a need that everyone has?* If not, it's likely to be one of many strategies for meeting a universal need.

For example, play is a need; a video game is one strategy to meet that need. Learning is a need; reading is one strategy for learning. Rest is a need; forcing your child to be in bed at eight o'clock is a strategy for meeting his need for rest, or yours. (See Keys 5 and 6 for more about needs and strategies.)

Explore Together: *Universal Needs List*

Make a list of universal needs and post it in the house where everyone can see it, refer to it, and add to it. This list provides a common vocabulary for respectful and compassionate communication, for understanding the motivations behind each of our actions, and for shared exploration of human needs. (For more about identifying needs, see "Needs List" and "Needs Mandala" in Part III, Topic: Family Meetings.)

▪ Feelings Are Helpful Messengers of Met and Unmet Needs

Feelings play an important role in your needs-messaging system. Feelings are like the panel on your dashboard: they alert you to whether your needs are being fulfilled or not. Pleasurable feelings such as *happy, satisfied*, and *joyful* give the message that needs are being fulfilled in that moment. Painful feelings like *sad, upset*, and *frustrated* give the message that some needs are not being fulfilled. Paying attention to your feelings and listening to their messages will give you important clues about your needs. Paying attention to the feelings of other people will give you important messages about how they are and, if you look further, about what they value or need.

Explore for Yourself

Think of a time when you felt joyful. What need was fulfilled that stimulated that feeling?

Think of a time when you felt frustrated or disappointed. What need was not fulfilled and was calling for your attention?

Think of a time when your child felt delighted. What need was being fulfilled at that time?

Think of a time when your child felt very sad. What need was not being fulfilled that gave rise to that sadness?

▪ Children Want to Be Heard and Understood

If your child lashes out at a sibling or at you, they are screaming, *I have some unmet needs!* Blaming or scolding them will only add to their pain. Instead, you can take time to listen respectfully to what's going on underneath their pain by hearing their feelings and needs. More than anything, children (and all people) want to be heard and understood for what's really going on.

When your child screams because another child took her toy, you could guess that she wants consideration or more control over her toys. Either of these guesses (whether silent guesses or out loud) will bring more connection with your child than if you judge her reactions as inappropriate, overreactive, or immature because you're thinking that she *should* share.

Seeing needs leads to more effective actions, while being blind to needs can lead to actions you may well regret. If you feel irritable and tired at the end of a day and recognize that you haven't eaten anything since breakfast, your need is most likely for nutrition. With this need clearly in mind, you can prepare something that will be nourishing. However, if you feel irritable and tired and don't look for the cause of those feelings, you might, without thinking, grab a candy bar or snap at your child.

Sadly, it is uncommon in our society to think in terms of feelings and needs. Few people have a vocabulary of feelings that extends beyond *mad, sad, glad,* and *frustrated,* and most people have been taught that having needs reflects badly on their character, that it indicates they are *selfish* or *needy*. A common belief is that a *strong* person doesn't need anything and a *good* person puts her or his needs last.

People who don't know that they have needs, who believe that it is unacceptable to have needs, and who have a limited vocabulary for talking about feelings and needs often act in ineffective and even destructive ways.

Explore for Yourself

Think of a time when you knew what you needed and chose to do something to meet that need.

What was the need?

What did you do to help meet your need?

How did you feel?

Think of a time when someone told you what would help them meet their need and you were willing and able to help.

What was their need?

What did you do to help meet their need?

How did you feel?

What needs of yours were met?

Summary

The fact that all behavior is an attempt to meet a need takes the mystery out of why children act the way they do and introduces a needs-focused approach to parenting. With this focus, parents can help kids learn to take more responsibility for meeting their own needs. Feelings are recognized as messages about whether or not needs are being fulfilled, and when parents have the skills to identify feelings, link them with the needs behind them, and strategize ways to meet them, children feel heard and understood.

Daily Practice

When you see the needs at the root of behavior, respect and co-operation will increase. While observing your children, your co-workers, or characters on TV, ask yourself, *What needs are they trying to meet with what they're doing?*

Observe your own actions and check to see what needs you are meeting. Ask yourself, *What needs am I trying to meet with what I'm doing?*

To develop an awareness of what's going on with you, at different times in the day, stop and ask yourself, *What am I feeling now? What needs are present?*

Love doesn't just sit there, like a stone; it has to be made, like bread, remade all the time, made new.

—Ursula K. LeGuin

Key 3 ▪ Create Safety, Trust, & Belonging

Key Concepts

▪ A child needs emotional safety to grow.

▪ Your actions affect your child's emotional safety.

▪ See from your child's point of view.

▪ To sustain emotional safety, seek connection—first, last, and always.

▪ To maintain safety, trust, and belonging, nurture family connections.

A child's presence is a gift he or she is giving to a parent. A parent's unconditional acceptance and appreciation for that gift completes the bonding process that is essential to an infant's sense of safety, trust, and belonging in the world. When needs for unconditional love and acceptance are met in infancy and early childhood, a message ripples through a young life to form a foundation of self-acceptance: *I am accepted by others; therefore, I can accept myself.*

Safety, trust, and belonging needs are met first by the family and then in an ever-widening arc that extends to peers at school, other community members, and eventually to co-workers and the larger world. With unconditional acceptance at home, kids are much more willing to learn from and be guided by their parents rather than try to meet needs for acceptance outside the home. Family substitutes such as cliques and gangs are usually last resorts for young people who are desperately trying to find a way to meet their need to belong, somewhere. The need to belong is so powerful that meeting these needs somewhere is much better than nowhere.

This key will show you ways to make home your child's number one place to belong.

> Your kids require you most of all to love them for who they are, not to spend your whole time trying to correct them.
>
> —Bill Ayers

▪ A Child Needs Emotional Safety to Grow

At the foundation of all human needs are those for food, water, shelter, and physical safety. These are indisputable needs the world over. Babies need to be dry and warm, well fed, clothed, and protected from physical harm, and they communicate their needs loudly. Creating safety and trust for your children, however, goes far beyond meeting physical needs.

Recent brain research establishes the importance of a less commonly recognized or talked-about safety requirement—the need for *emotional safety*. When infants or children of any age experience a physical or emotional threat, they become anxious and afraid. Hormones are secreted that automatically shut down the thinking, learning, and reasoning zones of the brain to prepare the child to defend himself or to run away from the danger.[1] These are very primitive fight, flight, or freeze responses that are triggered daily in the lives of children who don't feel safe. When, from very early ages, major portions of the brain shut down under emotionally stressful conditions, a child's brain development, success in learning, and ability to relate to others can be seriously affected.[2]

I have never met a person whose greatest need was anything other than real, unconditional love.

—Elisabeth Kübler-Ross

▪ Your Actions Affect Your Child's Emotional Safety

Some of the experiences that children interpret as dangerous include adults raising their voices, name-calling, comparing one child's mistakes with other children's successes, threatening punishment or consequences, shaking, hitting, and spanking. These highly charged ways of interacting cause children to question whether they are safe and secure with the people who care for them. Without a deep sense of safety and trust, they are cautious and hesitant about investigating their world. They are often full of self-doubt in the face of opportunities to explore and learn. They are often afraid to ask questions or take risks, and prefer a limited, safe range of options and strategies for meeting their needs.

When children feel emotionally safe, they are relaxed in their world

---

1. Daniel Goleman, *Emotional Intelligence.*
2. Allan Schore, *Affect Regulation and the Origin of the Self.*

and are excited to investigate it. They explore, ask questions, take risks, and remain open to a wide range of ways to meet vital needs.

Joseph Chilton Pearce and Michael Mendizza[3] take this point one giant step further. They say that it's not only what we do but also our state of mind and heart when we do it that children pick up on. They claim there is no difference between the state of one's consciousness and the environment created by that consciousness. If a mother prepares a meal for her family every evening, all the while feeling angry about what happened at work that day and resentful that she is spending so much time cooking instead of doing something more interesting and fun, what will her children learn from the experience of eating meals together? What will they learn if, instead, she sings a song and thinks about how cooking this meal meets her needs to nurture her family and spend time together? Whatever you do, children will remember most of all the state you're in—the quality of aliveness, the joy or lack of it.

■ See from Your Child's Point of View

Your kids want you to see them for who they are and what they can do. Recognition of their challenges and celebration of their accomplishments shows that you care and strengthens the bond of trust between you. To understand what needs are foremost and pressing at each stage of their lives, it is helpful to be aware of the developmental stages your kids are going through and to notice what is uniquely true about the child in front of you.

Understand Developmental Stages

An infant's brain is not fully developed at birth. In fact, it is now believed that some parts of the brain aren't fully formed until the early to mid-twenties. So we all grow into our adult thinking capacities at our own preprogrammed pace. Infants, toddlers, and preschoolers are self-absorbed

---

3. Mendizza and Pearce, *Magical Parent, Magical Child*.

and gradually develop the capacity to consider others. Developmentally they aren't ready to share toys, take turns, or to see another person's point of view. They have no way of understanding how long ten minutes or an hour is, and of course they have very few years of experience in the world to draw upon for making sound decisions.

If you expect adult thinking and behaviors before your child is developmentally ready to perform them, you threaten her sense of emotional security and undermine her ability and desire to trust you. Out of love for you, your toddler will make her best attempt to share toys or to understand another child's feelings; however, when she is unable to sustain her effort, she will feel confused and discouraged because she wants to do something she isn't yet developmentally able to do. Neither threats nor bribes can affect her actions. They only make her feel helpless that she can't do something you want her to do.

Trying to meet parents' expectations but not being ready to do so is a common experience for kids from infancy through their teens. Drinking from a cup, eating with a spoon, and tying shoes can't be done before brain and muscles are ready. A child expected to read before specific physical and conceptual readiness is in place may be excited to learn the skills. However, if he is judged or teased on his performance and called lazy or stupid for not doing well, he will feel discouraged. He is interested and smart; he just isn't ready for what is being asked of him.

Teens go through their own stages. They need consideration and respect for the challenges they face and their timetable for maturing. Many parents deal harshly with what they view as the poor judgment of their teens. Judgment, however, is a capacity that they grow. The young person's brain needs a chance to mature into making sound judgments. Teens need practice and a parent's patience with missteps along the way.

If you heed developmental cues and take your lead from your children about what they are ready to do, you will ensure that they will feel safe and ready for the next steps in their growth process.

Accept Your Child's Unique Personality and Learning Style

In addition to having a unique timetable for developing, children have their own unique personalities and ways of learning. Do you see your child as unique and accept her just the way she is?

It's natural to have an easier time raising one child than another. Many factors weigh in here. If a child is very different from you, it might be challenging to accept your differences. For example, if you enjoy reading, gardening, and doing other quiet activities and your child loves to have friends over, listen to music, make jokes, and be the center of attention, you may need to work at appreciating his style of expressing himself. If you have a child just like you, that could be challenging in a different way—wherever you turn, you hear and see yourself.

In any case, looking with respect to your child's needs will help you steer clear of dangerous labels such as *demanding, challenging, needy*, or *timid*. Labels get in the way of seeing your child and accepting him for the unique person he is.

As well as having a unique personality, your child has a particular set of requirements for optimum learning. Learning preferences show up early in life, and by observing closely you can discover the ways she learns best and make sure that her learning experiences are as successful as possible. Some kids learn best by listening to information, others from pictures and charts. For many kids, talking about or teaching what they're learning makes learning come alive, and still others do best when making models, drawing, or getting their whole body involved and acting things out. All of these learning styles can be understood and worked with.

Observe your child carefully, experiment with different ways of interacting with her, and find a comfort zone for working together. And when your child approaches school age, do be aware that there are many ways to learn in addition to those typically used in schools (which are often limited to reading textbooks, writing reports, and memorizing words on a spelling list). Get help, if you need it, to create a learning environment that supports your child in being a successful, lifelong learner.[4]

> The more we witness our emotional chain reactions and understand how they work, the easier it is to refrain. It becomes a way of life to stay awake, slow down, and notice.
>
> —Pema Chodron

---

4. For more information on learning styles, see Hodson and Willis, *Discover Your Child's Learning Style*.

▪ To Sustain Emotional Safety, Seek Connection— First, Last, and Always

The feeling of satisfaction and contentment that comes from being connected to an accepting, caring adult is essential for children to thrive.

Parents tell us it is challenging to make heartfelt connections with their kids when there are so many interactions in a day and days move by so swiftly. When they don't take time to connect, they report that interactions often end in compromise, discord, and fuel for future arguments. Feelings of sadness, anger, discouragement, and hopelessness run high. These same parents tell us that they feel great relief when they do take time at the moment (at least some moments) to listen to and attempt to understand their kids, the situation, and themselves. The extra time they give to one stressful interaction results in more ease and less time spent down the road in similar challenging interactions.

Most often, the quickest route to connection with your child is to listen respectfully to what he has to say, tuning into the feelings and needs he is trying to share in whatever way he happens to be expressing them in that moment. He is always trying to communicate only two things—how he feels and what he needs. Expressing honestly how you feel and what you need is also part of making a genuine connection. However, for optimum connection, listening to your child first is most helpful.

Look for listening opportunities. Some parents find long car drives make for easy talking and listening. Some make a point of scheduling one-on-one time with each child. When kids can count on opportunities to express themselves and to be heard, they are less likely to nag and whine and can relax, knowing you will make time to hear them.

Let Go of Resentment

When you go through rough patches and feelings get hurt, connection sometimes gets broken. It's crucial to reestablish the loving tie between you and your child as soon as possible. When you reestablish connection, you inspire confidence in your child that he is okay, he can make mistakes and people will still love him, and he doesn't have to be perfect to be loved. Each time you reconnect with your child during or after an argument you not only reestablish the trust and safety link, you strengthen it. When kids realize you will always seek to reconnect, interactions will get easier, you'll spend much less time at odds with each other, and strategies for working out problems will become more evident, sooner.

Young children tend to reconnect a lot faster than adults do. Take a tip from them: one minute your kids might feel sad and dejected, the next they are energized and excited. They may have outbursts of emotion; however, they get over them quickly and don't hold grudges. They let go of the past with startling speed and bounce back with freshness and openness for whatever is next. This is a wonderful gift of consideration and trust that they are continually giving to you.

Children are anxious to receive the same consideration from you. However, the habit of holding on to hurt is deeply ingrained in adults. This common habit prevents parents from seeing the more positive side of their children's behavior and eventually prevents children from wanting to express it. Since holding a grudge is something that is learned somewhere between childhood and adulthood, the good news is, it can be unlearned.

After you've had a disagreement with a child, see how long it takes you to let go of your judgments and bad feelings. After the next distressing situation, see if you can let go a little faster. Keep it light, keep it fun, and watch your kids for pointers. The more you keep focused on everyone's feelings and needs, the easier letting go becomes.

> Listening is an attitude of the heart, a genuine desire to be with another which both attracts and heals.
>
> —J. Isham

Listen for the *Yes* Behind Every *No*

What you do when your children resist or refuse to do what you tell them affects their sense of safety and trust. When your child digs in her heels and says *No!* do you see her action as a call to arms? Do you get angry and defensive and want to persuade her to change her mind by preaching to her or punishing her?

No might be the most charged word in the parenting dictionary. Lots and lots of parent hours and energy are spent battling children who say *No. No* is an unacceptable response because parents are uncomfortable with each of the choices they think they have when they hear it. They think they have to either accept the *No* and change their position or refuse to accept the *No* and find a way for the child to change her position.

Parents can save themselves hours of hassle by understanding that there is a third way to hear *No*: this is to hear a *Yes* behind every *No*. Whenever your child says *No* to you, he is saying *Yes* to something else. By taking time to find out what is more exciting, interesting, fun, or challenging than what you have in mind, you defuse a potentially volatile situation, make a heartfelt connection, and clearly demonstrate your interest and care.

In this example, the parent is able to hear the *Yes* behind her child's *No*. Mom walks into her son's room, where he is reading a book:

Mom: *Since Dad's away, I'd like to spend some extra time with you this weekend. Would you like to go to a movie with me tonight?*

Son: *No, I'm busy.*

Mom: (Looking for the *Yes* behind the *No*) *Looks as if you are really absorbed in that book.*

Son: *Yeah. It is really getting good.*

Mom: (Realizing her son needs choice, relaxation, and alone time) *Sounds like tonight you'd rather keep reading.*

Son: *Yeah! Maybe I can finish it.*

Mom: (Not giving up on her need) *I'm still interested in a movie or doing something else together on another night. How does that sound to you?*

Son: *Fine. How about Sunday night? I know I'll be finished by then.*

> When we know ourselves to be connected to all others, acting compassionately is simply the natural thing to do.
>
> —Rachel Naomi Remen

Imagine what would have happened if Mom had reacted when her son said, *No, I'm busy*, taking it as a rejection. She might have said, *Well, you have time for other things*, or *What's more important, a book or your mother?* or *I didn't think it was much to ask of you.* She would likely have lost connection with her son and also lost her chance for a movie date with him.

Next time your child says *No!*—notice your reactions. Then see if you can hear what need she is saying *Yes* to. Hear the *Yes* behind the *No* and you will both sustain the connection between you and be open to seeing the best way to meet your own needs.

▪ To Maintain Safety, Trust, and Belonging, Nurture Family Connections

If improved family communication is what you want, you need a place where family members regularly practice their skills. At the same time that improving daily interactions between you and your children nurtures your one-on-one relationships, holding family meetings serves needs to harmonize your family unit.

Hold Family Meetings

Family meetings are hours set aside to plan family events, share concerns, identify feelings and needs, find ways to fulfill needs, celebrate personal victories, set household and individual goals, take stock, and strategize solutions to problems.

Be sure to make an agreement for your meetings that ensures safety and trust for everyone. Each member of the group can contribute what she or he needs to feel safe in these meetings. Keep the list at hand and read it at the beginning of each meeting. The following are some strategies for meeting safety needs that parents and kids have shared with us: the right to participate by just listening; no suggestions or advice given without first asking if the other person wants to hear it; assurance that there will be no name-calling, threats, criticism, blame, or loud voices.

(For ways to set up family meetings, co-create agreements, and enjoy activities with your family, see Part III, Topic: Family Meetings.)

Summary

In addition to physical safety, children need emotional safety to trust that the world is a welcoming place. Parents' actions and reactions greatly affect whether a child feels emotionally safe or not. When parents learn to see from a child's point of view, to strengthen the bond of parent-child connection whenever possible, and to create a forum for nourishing the family unit, children will feel relaxed and free to explore and enjoy their world.

Daily Practice

Notice your actions and reactions. Ask yourself, *Does this contribute to emotional safety and trust?*

Notice how much you talk and how much you listen. Make time to listen.

In interactions with your child, ask yourself, *Am I going for connection? Or something else?*

Practice hearing the *Yes* behind the *No*. First, notice when your child says *No*. Notice your automatic reactions. Look for the need your child is saying *Yes* to in that moment.

Heart Rhythm Resonance

A growing body of neurocardiological research finds that infants sense and resonate with the coherency or incoherency of the rhythms of an adult's heart.[1] Feelings of irritation, frustration, and anger lead to a disordered and incoherent pattern of heart rhythms in the body. Feelings of appreciation, enjoyment, compassion, and love lead to more ordered and coherent heart rhythm patterns.[2] And, the heart rhythms of one person entrain the heart rhythms of another.[3] Therefore, parents' emotional responses, even though nonverbal, can determine their child's own emotional responses and behaviors.[4] A caregiver's emotional state and the quality of nurturing and care an infant receives have a significant effect on brain development and other factors that determine whether a child will thrive or not.

---

1. Siegel and Hartzell, *Parenting from the Inside Out.*
2. Childre and Rozman, *The HeartMath Solution.*
3. Pearce, *The Biology of Transcendence.*
4. Siegel and Hartzell, *Parenting from the Inside Out.*

Key 4 ▪ Inspire Giving

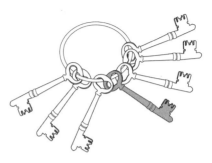

Key Concepts

- Giving is a fundamental human need.
- You and your children have many gifts to give.
- Receive your child's gifts.
- Give your gifts freely.
- Learn from your child's gift of liveliness.

Co-operation, or *operating together,* implies that all parties have something to share. Even at very early ages, children have a surprisingly delightful ability to share with parents. By recognizing the gifts your children have to give and by developing the skills to gratefully receive them, you meet deep needs for contribution for you and your children that affect the core of self-worth for each of you.

▪ Giving Is a Fundamental Human Need

Your children have a need to contribute to your well-being and to the well-being of the family as a whole. As we see it, a primary parental role is to inspire giving—to help young people understand what they have to share and how they can share it in a way that it can be received. Of course, to inspire this give-and-take means to actively value a mutual exchange and actively find ways for children to contribute to the stream of giving. Handing kids a list of chores to do and telling them when they need to be completed doesn't inspire giving—nor do threats, punishments, or rewards.

Giving comes naturally to human beings when it isn't forced. In fact, giving may be the source of the greatest joy possible. Simple acts of heartfelt giving are continually taking place in a family: Parents get up

> Giving makes the other person a giver also, and they both share in the joy of what they have brought to life. In the act of giving lies the expression of my aliveness.
>
> —Eric Fromm

night after night to comfort and feed their newborn infant. A child rushes home from school with a colorfully wrapped present she has made in preschool and excitedly places it on her dad's favorite chair. Family members gather in the kitchen to make dinner together.

▪ You and Your Children Have Many Gifts to Give

Everyone, including children, possesses a wealth of ideas, talents, skills, and fruits of their interests that they can share. Some people give their singing, some give vegetables from their garden, some give cookies, some give poems or paintings. Even if all personal skills and talents were set aside, there are some things that we all can give: time, energy, attention, listening, or even a smile. Just sitting in the same room with someone who is ill can be helpful, so sharing time can be a gift. When a family member has a big job to do, lending a helping hand is a gift. When a friend is in distress, attention and listening can be a gift. When children are sad or scared, sometimes just holding them is the gift.

> A bird doesn't sing because it has an answer, it sings because it has a song.
>
> —Maya Angelou

From the moment they are born, infants are bursting with their own kinds of gifts to give, including their warmth, their trusting gaze, and their smiles. Children of all ages continually offer their playful spirits, laughter, inquisitiveness, honesty, affection, and humor. If parents are able to recognize and receive these gifts, their children will grow up knowing what powerful givers they are and how happy they feel when what they have to give is received.

If children have so many gifts to give, why is it common to hear parents complaining about how little their children do around the house? There are many roadblocks to kids contributing: Many don't think they have anything to give. Parents often fail to recognize that contributions need to be made willingly. Parents often focus on the negative and don't take time to acknowledge the positive contributions their children make. Many parents are fixed on their own agenda of what, when, and how kids *should* contribute.

Here's a story about one parent who took time to recognize and receive the gift his son was offering him. Dad was rushing to get himself and his six-year-old son, Josh, dressed and out the door so he could get Josh to school and get himself to work on time. When, instead of putting on his socks, Josh started jumping up and down with excitement and began telling his dad a joke he had just made up, Dad immediately felt irritated and was about to say, *Come on, we don't have time for jokes. We have to go, NOW!* but caught himself before he took this route. He knew that if he delivered this message it would only create more stress for both of them. He stopped, took a breath, and said, *Josh, I see how excited you are to tell me your joke, and I want to hear it. I love laughing with you, and I'd like it if you could tell me the joke when I can be relaxed enough to really listen and enjoy it, like in the car. Would you get dressed fast and then tell the joke in the car?* Josh was able to do this. And while this approach doesn't always work out as smoothly as in this example, taking time to receive a child's gift instead of pushing him aside always works in the long run.

Explore for Yourself

Make a list of some of the gifts your children give.

1._____

2._____

3._____

4._____

5._____

6._____

7._____

■ Receive Your Child's Gifts

Willingness to receive is an additional gift parents have to give to their kids. Receiving a gift with heartfelt acknowledgement and genuine appreciation generates a flow of goodwill between giver and receiver.

The need to contribute to the well-being of others is somewhat like a muscle; you use it or risk losing it. Without exercise a muscle sags and eventually atrophies. And when failing to have gifts recognized and received, a child becomes discouraged and loses her desire to give.

By noticing and receiving your children's spontaneous actions as gifts, you save your kids from believing that *gifts* refer only to items bought in stores. In a society that often equates wealth with money, young people often see themselves as useless and powerless to give to others as long as they don't have lots of money to buy things. When you acknowledge the gifts your children give freely, they will grow up seeing themselves as powerful givers. As a natural outcome of having their gifts received, they are more likely to recognize and appreciate the steady stream of gifts you give them.

Some ways you can let your children know that you receive their gifts are to share how you feel about receiving what is being offered and to share what need of yours was met by receiving the gift. *When you gave me that big smile this morning as you went out the door to school, I felt very happy. I love those quick moments of connection.*

> The greatest gift we can give to our children is not just to share our riches with them, but to reveal their riches to themselves.
>
> —Swahili proverb

Explore for Yourself

Think of ways you give from the heart. Make a list of ways or things you can give others (that don't cost money).

Make a list of things you receive from others (that don't cost money).

Explore Together: *Celebrating Gifts*

Invite everyone in your family to write or draw about the gifts each has
to give. You can help each other think of these gifts. The gifts can all be
listed on one page or you can put one gift on each page and illustrate it.
Compile the pages in a three-ring binder and give it a title such as *Family
Book of Gifts*. Add to it as new gifts come to mind. Let the book serve as
a source of gratitude and a reminder that each member of the family has
the power to contribute.

Explore Together: *Notes of Appreciation*

Make several photocopies of the notes of appreciation found in Part III
("Note of Appreciation" in Topic: Life-Enriching Practices) and keep a
stack of them near the dining-room table.

Fill out notes before a dinner, fold them, and place them on your
child's napkin.

■ Give Your Gifts Freely

The best things in life are free. They don't cost money; however, and more
importantly, they are freely given—no strings attached. Giving freely,
without any expectation of getting anything back or any sense of obligation, guilt, or fear, primes the pump for others to give freely to you. And
the result in such willing exchanges is that the giver and the receiver both
feel great joy and genuine connection.

This joy in giving is greatly diminished if you expect something in
return. The flow of heartfelt connection is also absent if there is a sense
of obligation that you *must* give, *ought to* give, or *should* give.

If you find yourself feeling resentful, it is likely there are some strings
attached to your giving. Maybe you are overcommitted and need to cut
back on the number of things you do. Maybe you think you should be
doing things you could ask or hire someone else to do. Maybe your standards for how things should be done keep you busier than you need to be.

Explore for Yourself

Think of a specific time you gave to someone just because you wanted to.

What did you give?

What needs did this meet for the other person?

What needs did this meet for you?

How did you feel when giving just because you wanted to?

Explore for Yourself

Giving connects
two people,
the giver and
the receiver,
and this
connection
gives birth to
a new sense
of belonging.

—Deepak Chopra

Think of a specific time you gave to someone because you thought you should.

What did you give?

What needs did this meet for the other person?

What needs did this meet for you?

How did you feel when giving because you thought you should?

Explore Together: *Giving from the Heart*

Family members take turns sharing about times during the day that they gave freely to others or to themselves.

Discuss the needs met for the person who received the gift as well as the needs met for the giver.

Draw a picture of the giving event and share the pictures with each other.

Notice all the different ways to give.

Notice how you feel when you give just because you want to give.

▪ Learn from Your Child's Gift of Liveliness

In some ways your children are as much guides for your life as you are for theirs. It is our belief that kids come into parents' lives to be a source of inspiration and a reminder of how lively and engaging life can be. For children the world is a giant laboratory, and they are very serious explorers of it. Watch, experiment with them, and learn from them because they can help you remember how to be deeply in love with life.

Children play and explore, laugh and wonder right out loud. They provide a constant invitation for us to join them. Accept their invitation and cross the line into their world. Take as much spirit and willingness with you as you want them to bring to your world. Let them be your eyes and ears. Imagine how it must feel to walk through sand for the first time, to balance on two wheels and zoom through space, to pluck petals from a daisy and sense the flower slightly tugging back, to hear an airplane or the wind or a crow caw for the first time. Their awe can be yours. They are willing and waiting to share it with you.

Your teens can remind you how painful and awkward you once felt in social situations, just the way they are feeling now. They can help you remember how bored you were by homework and how excited and scared you were when you went on your first date. Your willingness to allow your teens to remind you of what it was like to be a teen is your link with their life as they are now living it, and with their heart.

> The hardest battle is to be nobody but yourself in a world that is doing its best, night and day, to make you like everybody else.
>
> —e. e. cummings

Summary

Contributing to the well-being of others is a fundamental need, even for children. When parents recognize and receive the gifts children have to give, they inspire the child's natural desire to give. Children are always giving of themselves—their liveliness, their laughter, and their love. Parents are invited to receive this precious gift and learn from it.

Daily Practice

Notice and acknowledge the gifts your child is offering.

Find ways for your child to experience herself or himself as a powerful giver.

Notice when you are giving if the giving is free or if there are strings attached.

Children need
to be enjoyed
and valued, not
managed.

—Daniel J. Siegel

Key 5 ▪ Use a Language of Respect

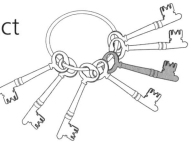

Key Concepts

- Remember your intention.
- Notice the flow of communication.
- Make clear observations—free of evaluations.
- Connect with feelings and needs.
- Make do-able requests.
- Listen with empathy.

How many times have you said something to your child and then wished you could have erased those words?

How often have you said, *I didn't mean to say that!* or *I don't know where that came from!*

How many times have you experienced some instant recognition: *That sounded just like my mother when she got mad!*

Language matters! Words can incite and fuel conflict. They also have the power to engender respect and understanding and inspire co-operation. The good news is that you can greatly enhance your ability to connect with your kids if you learn and practice language that does not judge, criticize, blame, or demand but instead keeps a respectful focus on needs.

Everything in this book is about establishing ways of thinking, listening, and acting that lead to a more conscious and respectful use of language. This key focuses in particular on the specific components of Nonviolent Communication (NVC). Learning these skills will serve you in a couple of ways: You will be able to transform judgments, blame, criticism, and demands into respectful, compassionate ways of thinking and

> The objective of Nonviolent Communication is not to change people and their behavior in order to get our way: it is to establish relationships based on honesty and empathy which will eventually fulfill everyone's needs.
>
> —Marshall B. Rosenberg

seeing. You will also be guided in how to respectfully listen to others and how to honestly and respectfully express yourself.

This language of respect is called by many names, including Nonviolent Communication, compassionate communication, effective communication, and the language of the heart. It is also called Giraffe Language for learning and for fun. The giraffe was chosen as a symbol because of its large heart (twenty-six pounds!) and because of its long neck, which allows for a broad perspective. In contrast, the way of thinking and speaking that judges, blames, criticizes, finds fault, and makes demands is referred to as Jackal Language. Bear in mind that these metaphors are meant to be convenient and fun terms that refer to two kinds of thinking, not labels to support a belief that there are two kinds of people. Anyone can be susceptible to Jackal thinking, listening, and talking. As well, anyone can begin now to learn a new language of connection and respect. (For more about Giraffe and Jackal, see the information in Part III, Topic: Giraffe & Jackal Culture.)

▪ Remember Your Intention

Words matter. However, intention is still 90 percent of communication. Without a clear and conscious intention to connect, even the most skillfully crafted expression can be heard as hollow or manipulative. Remember that the sole intention of Giraffe Language is to make a heartfelt connection with oneself and with others—and to respect and care for everyone's needs.

Use these questions to check your intentions in any interaction:

Do I want to connect right now?

Or do I want to be right and get my way?

If you want to be right and get your way, you aren't yet ready to make a connection with another person. (See the Communication Flow Chart in this key.)

Explore for Yourself

In your own words, write down your intention.

What do you want to create in your relationship with your children?

What is your intention for your next interaction with your child?

Take time to nourish your intention. It's all too easy to stay with your nose down to the ground, responding and reacting to the steady stream of daily interactions with your children and with everyone else. Making a habit of regularly nourishing your intention will help you remember it more regularly throughout your busy days, and especially when you need it the most!

Learning and practicing Giraffe Language will help nourish your intention. Other ways to nourish your intention include the following: taking a moment in the morning, before the day begins, to remember your intention; breathing deeply in the middle of an intense interaction and giving yourself empathy; taking time to be in nature; reading inspirational books; meditating; praying; singing; dancing; writing; drawing; and painting.

> **Our language habits are at the core of how we imagine the world.**
>
> —Neil Postman

Communication Flow Chart

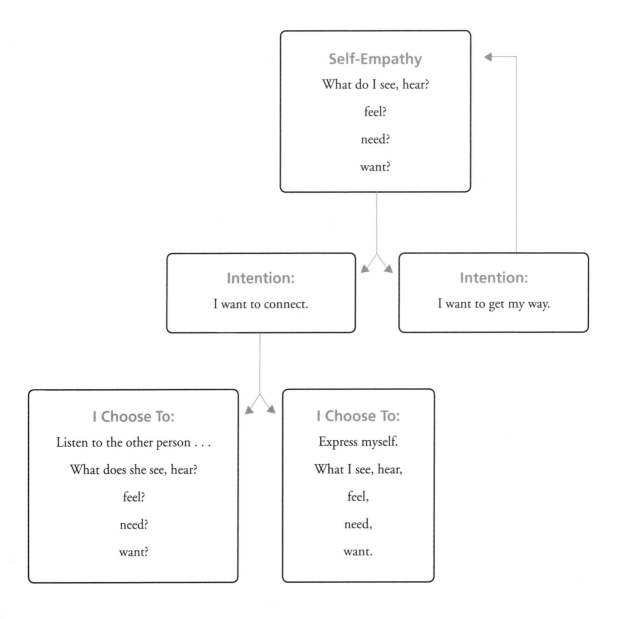

Self-Empathy

What do I see, hear?

feel?

need?

want?

Intention:

I want to connect.

Intention:

I want to get my way.

I Choose To:

Listen to the other person . . .

What does she see, hear?

feel?

need?

want?

I Choose To:

Express myself.

What I see, hear,

feel,

need,

want.

▪ Notice the Flow of Communication

In any dialogue, there is a kind of traffic flow: sometimes you express and sometimes you listen. It helps to step back at times and notice who's talking and who's listening. Have you noticed that when you and your child are talking at the same time, no one really gets heard? In order for each of you to be heard, someone will have to step back, from time to time, and listen. Giraffe Language will show you how to do this important listening without giving in or giving up what you, also, want to say.

When you are aware of the flow of communication, you have more choice about where to focus your attention. You can choose one of three ways of interacting: *listening* with self-empathy to your feelings and needs; *listening* with empathy to the other person's feelings and needs; or *expressing* your honest feelings and needs. Giraffe Language suggests you choose where to focus based on where you are likely to find the most connection.

For example, if your daughter is too upset to hear what you have to say, the most connection will be found when you listen to her. Or, if you are too upset to hear her feelings and needs, the most connection will likely be found when you, first, listen to what's going on in you.

As well as guiding you in *where* to focus your attention, Giraffe Language gives clear guidelines for *what* to focus on. There are three items on the list: (1) make clear observations—free of evaluations, (2) connect with feelings and needs, and (3) make do-able requests. These components of Giraffe Language are introduced, step by step, in the following pages. This is a very brief introduction and there is much more to learn and practice. More resources, including books, tapes, videos, and workshops, can be found at www.cnvc.org or www. NonviolentCommunication.org.

> What I want in my life is compassion, a flow between myself and others based on a mutual giving from the heart.
>
> —Marshall B. Rosenberg

Giraffe Expressing

I say as honestly as I can: My Observations,
Feelings, Needs, and Requests.

Observations	I say what I see and hear. *When I hear . . .*
Feelings	I say how I feel. *I feel . . .*
Needs	I say what I need. *Because I need . . .*
Requests	I ask for what I predict will meet my needs. *Right now I would like . . . If you are willing . . .*

Giraffe Listening / Empathy

I make my best guesses about: Your Observations,
Feelings, Needs, and Requests.

I guess what you see and hear. **Observations**
When you see/hear . . .

I guess your feelings. **Feelings**
Do you feel . . .

I guess your needs. **Needs**
Because you need . . . ?

I guess what might help **Requests**
you meet your needs.
Right now would you like . . . ?

▪ Make Clear Observations—Free of Evaluations

The first step in expressing yourself in Giraffe is to clearly describe what it is you are reacting to. Your ability to make observations free of evaluations will serve you greatly in connecting with your kids. For instance, if you say to your son, *You were very rude this morning*, he is likely to hear this as a criticism and want to defend himself, either by arguing or shutting down. If, instead, you make a clear observation of what happened, your son will more likely stay to hear more. A clear observation sounds like this: *When I said Hi to you this morning, you looked the other way.*

To develop the skill of making clear observations, free of evaluations, pretend you are looking through the lens of a video camera. What, precisely, do you see (or hear or remember)? When you use vivid and evaluation-free observations, you take a first step toward connection with your child and open the door to further dialogue.

Explore for Yourself

Imagine your reaction to hearing each of the following statements. Keep in mind that the speaker's tone of voice and posture are also communicating the message behind the words.

> *You never listen.* (evaluation)
>
> *I see you looking in your book while I'm talking to you.* (clear observation)
>
> *You're being lazy.* (evaluation)
>
> *It's ten o'clock and you're still in bed.* (clear observation)
>
> *You're irresponsible.* (evaluation)
>
> *You said you'd feed the dog tonight and I see that the can of food is unopened.* (clear observation)

To observe
without
evaluation
is the highest
form of human
intelligence.

—J. Krishnamurti

Needs List

We all need:

Fun

Play

Learning

Choices

Physical Nurturance

> Air, exercise, food, protection, rest, sexual expression, shelter, touch, water

Relationship with Ourself

> Achievement, acknowledgement, authenticity, challenges, clarity, competence, creativity, integrity, knowing our gifts and talents, meaning, privacy, self-development, self-expression, self-worth

Relationship with Others

> Appreciation, belonging, to share life's joys and sorrows, closeness, community, consideration, emotional safety, empathy, honesty, interdependence, kindness, love, power-with, reassurance, respect, sharing gifts and talents, support, to matter to someone, trust, understanding, warmth

Relationship with the World

> Beauty, contact with nature, harmony, inspiration, order, peace

This Needs List is not intended to be complete; we encourage you to add to it and refine it.

Feelings List

When Needs Are Met	When Needs Are Not Met
Comfortable, full, satisfied, at ease, relaxed, safe	**Uncomfortable**, uneasy, irritable, unsafe, miserable, embarrassed
Rested, refreshed, energized, alert, relaxed, alive, strong	**Tired**, exhausted, sleepy, dull, weak, foggy, dead
Interested, curious, excited	**Uninterested**, bored, blah
Glad, happy, hopeful, grateful, delighted, jazzed, cheerful	**Sad**, unhappy, disappointed, heavy, lonely, gloomy, bummed
Peaceful, calm, clear, content	**Nervous**, worried, confused, tense
Loving, connected, warm, open, tender, friendly, affectionate	**Mad**, angry, irritated, frustrated, upset, furious, hostile
Grateful, appreciative, thankful	**Annoyed**, disappointed, bitter
Playful, adventurous, alive, inspired, stimulated, eager	**Scared**, afraid, hesitant, shocked, fearful, worried, terrified, stuck

This Feelings List is a resource for expanding and enriching a feeling vocabulary. We suggest that you and your family add to it. For a more extensive list of feeling words, refer to *Nonviolent Communication: A Language of Life* by Marshall Rosenberg or to the Feelings List at www.cnvc.org.

■ Connect with Feelings and Needs

After a clear observation, express your feelings and your needs. The consciousness of needs is at the heart of Giraffe Language. Remember that needs are what connect us because they are the same for everyone, regardless of age, custom, ethnicity, or whether you are a parent or a child. When your focus is on needs, whether expressing or listening, you facilitate greater understanding and connection.

Feelings are the helpful messengers pointing to your needs. When needs are being met you will experience feelings such as happy, excited, and satisfied. Feelings of sadness, worry, frustration, and irritability tell you that your needs are not being met. What a great system to help you attend to your needs! Feelings also point you in the direction of your child's needs. In this regard, all feeling messages are helpful.

Your feelings, then, are rooted in your needs. Your child's feelings have their roots in his or her needs. Your daughter feels scared when her need for safety is not being met. She is likely to feel lonely or sad when her need for friendship isn't met. She can feel excited and proud when her need for accomplishment is met. Giraffe Language helps you express the truth about your feelings and what causes them. Note that feelings are never caused by other people, so phrases such as *You make me happy* or *She makes me angry* are not used in Giraffe Language.

The grammar of Giraffe Language makes this responsibility for feelings very clear: When expressing in Giraffe, you say *I feel _____ because I need _____*. And when listening to your children (or anyone else), you guess what they are feeling and needing: *Do you feel _____ because you need _____?*

I feel relieved ***because I needed*** *understanding, and I got it.*

I feel worried ***because I need*** *trust that you'll be okay.*

I feel grateful ***because I needed*** *support, and you are giving that to me right now.*

Do you feel *frustrated* ***because you*** *need to be listened to?*

Are you feeling upset **because you** *would like more choice in this matter?*

Are you feeling delighted **because you** *got to play all day?*

(See Key 2 for more about feelings and needs.)

Transforming Anger

Strong feelings of annoyance, intense irritation, and, especially, anger most often mean that there are thoughts mixed up with and adding fire to your feelings. These thoughts are about what you believe other people are doing to you or what you believe they *should* be doing. You and your children can learn to transform anger by shifting the energy of anger, recognizing the anger-producing thoughts, and hearing the needs-serving message beneath the anger. (For a step-by-step exercise on transforming anger, see "Transform Anger" in Part III, Topic: Life-Enriching Practices.)

▪ Make Do-able Requests

When you know what your needs are and can express them, you can then make clear requests about what people can do to help meet your needs.

Giraffe Language guides you in telling people what specific action they can do to help you now. A request, to be effective, must be do-able. The following three examples are do-able requests, asking for specific actions within a specific time frame:

Would you be willing to take ten minutes and help me pick up the living room?

Right now, would you brainstorm with me some ways to help you remember to wash your hands before eating?

Would you be willing to lower your voice for the next ten minutes while I'm on the phone?

The following are examples of non do-able requests.

Would you help around the house?

Will you remember to wash your hands before eating from now on?

Would you be more considerate?

How to Tell a Feeling from a Thought

Feelings are expressed most simply and clearly using just three words. For example, *I feel sad, I feel worried, I feel excited, I feel happy*. While feelings are a vital component of Giraffe Language, they are nearly absent in Jackal Language. Jackal Language is head-talk and steers clear of the concerns and the vulnerability of the heart. Instead, it focuses almost exclusively on thoughts, opinions, and judgments. At times these are even couched in feeling language, which contributes to misunderstanding and confusion. An example of this is *I feel that's unfair*. *Unfair* is not a word that describes a feeling; it is a thought that expresses an evaluation. In the following examples of Jackal Language, notice that though the word *feel* is used, we don't know how the speaker is really feeling:

I feel that you're inconsiderate.

I feel like I don't matter.

I feel it's not right.

In each of the above statements it would be more accurate to replace the phrase *I feel* with the phrase *I think*. When you identify your thoughts, you may notice you have feelings attached:

When I think that you're inconsiderate, I feel angry.

When I think that I don't matter, I feel sad and angry.

When I think that it's not right, I feel angry.

Even though the following phrases have the word *feel* in them, notice that they are actually going to express thoughts, judgments, or evaluations:

I feel like . . .

I feel that . . .

I feel it . . .

I feel as if . . .

I feel you/he/she/they . . .

Thoughts Posing as Feelings Lead to Anger

Anger-producing thoughts often pose as feelings. For example people say, *I feel manipulated*, or *I feel insulted*. Manipulated and insulted, however, are not feelings. They are thoughts about what you think others are doing to you. It is more accurate to say, *I think you are manipulating me and when I think that thought, I feel angry! I also feel sad and scared; I want to trust that you care about me.*

These words are all anger-producing thoughts: abandoned, attacked, blamed, betrayed, cornered, criticized, dissed, dumped on, ignored, insulted, intimidated, invalidated, left out, let down, manipulated, misunderstood, neglected, patronized, pressured, put down, rejected, ripped off, smothered, threatened, tricked, unheard, unimportant, unseen, and used.

Requests vs. Demands

How do you know if you've made a request and not a demand? Expressing your needs and making requests for something that is do-able now increases the likelihood that your child will want to help you meet that need. However, at the time you make your request there may be other needs your child is wanting to meet that will lead them to say *No* to your request. What you feel and what you say next will demonstrate whether you have made a request or a demand. If you are upset on hearing *No* to your request, you have probably made a demand. If you have made a request, you can receive your child's *No* as another possible point of connection. (See Key 3 to learn more about how to hear the *Yes* behind every *No*.)

▪ Listen with Empathy

Empathy is a respectful understanding of what someone is experiencing. It requires giving full attention to the inner experience of feelings and needs and putting aside for the time being your own judgments, opinions, and fears. To listen with empathy takes practice, since automatic responses of advising, lecturing, and commiserating are common. While these non-empathic responses are not considered bad, our experience confirms that what people want first and most, especially when they are in pain, is empathy. That's why Giraffe Language advises you to Give Empathy First.

You can listen with empathy to others and you can listen with empathy to yourself. In many cases, in order to be able to listen with empathy to others, you will first need to empathize with yourself.

Listening to Yourself: Self-Empathy

Giraffe Language encourages you to develop the habit of frequently checking in with what is going on with you—noticing your ever-changing feelings and needs. When you do this, you meet your need for self-connection and self-respect and you will feel more alive and present. You will also find yourself engaged in productive, energizing, needs-meeting actions more of the time.

Giraffe Self-Empathy

I say to *myself*: My Observations, Feelings, Needs, and Requests.

I say what I see and hear.
When I see/hear . . .

I say what I feel.
I feel . . .

I say what I need.
Because I need . . .

I decide what I think
might meet my needs.
Right now I ask myself to . . .

When you feel painful feelings—upset, hurt, worried, angry—taking the time to connect with your feelings and needs often meets your needs for comfort, understanding, and compassion. When you feel confused, listening to your thoughts and inner dialogue can create clarity.

When you feel pleasurable feelings—happy, excited, joyful, satisfied—self-empathy is a way to privately acknowledge and celebrate needs that have been met. Whenever you acknowledge that your needs have been met, you build confidence in your ability to meet needs in the future.

Examples of Self-Empathy

> *When I think of how I used such a loud voice with the kids today, I feel sad and disappointed because I didn't create the connection with them that I wanted. It also didn't meet my need for respect.*
>
> *When I see how difficult it is for me to stay focused on my work and my family, I feel concerned and worried because I need to be healthy and present for things that matter.*

Listening to Others: Empathy

More than anything, your kids want to be heard. Listening to them with a focus on their feelings and needs is the essence of empathy. Empathy is giving the gift of your presence—without judgment, analysis, suggestions, stories, or any motivation to fix things. When you empathize with your children you listen for their feelings and needs even, and especially, when their words sound like criticism, blame, or judgment.

Empathy is not dependent on words; it is, in fact, often silent. If it seems helpful to express empathy out loud, it's important to guess rather than state the other person's feelings and needs. Guessing shows a respectful understanding that you never know for sure what others' feel and need. Respectful guessing sounds like this: *Are you feeling frustrated and wish this puzzle was easier? Are you worried and do you want reassurance you'll be safe?*

> Empathy is a respectful understanding of what others are experiencing. Instead of offering empathy, we often have a strong urge to give advice or reassurance and to explain our own position or feeling. Empathy, however, calls upon us to empty our mind and listen to others with our whole being.
>
> —Marshall B. Rosenberg

Being accurate in your guessing is not important. Being sincerely interested in what's going on with your child is. Taking time to let go of your own agenda and be fully present to what's going on in your child is a golden gift, and the surest route to connection.

Examples of Non-Empathic Responses

These are some common, non-empathic responses that are unlikely to meet your needs at times when connection is the goal:

Advising:	*I think you should . . .*
Commiserating:	*That's terrible. She had no right to do that to you.*
Consoling:	*Everything's going to be okay.*
Correcting:	*It's not really that hard.*
Educating:	*You can learn from this.*
Explaining:	*I didn't want to do it this way, but . . .*
Evaluating:	*If you hadn't been so careless . . .*
Fixing:	*What will help you is to . . .*
Interrogating:	*What are you feeling? When did you start feeling this way?*
One-upping:	*You should hear what happened to me . . .*
Shutting down:	*Don't worry. It will go away.*
Story-telling:	*Your story reminds me of the time . . .*
Sympathizing:	*You poor thing.*

Summary

Learning Giraffe is a lot like learning a foreign language: it takes study and practice over time to develop fluency. At first, as you become more aware of your language habits and begin to practice, you might feel tongue-tied and awkward. At times, you may even begin to doubt that it is possible to unlearn habitual ways of speaking and listening. At those times, we hope you will remember that knowing even a little bit of a foreign language will increase your ability to communicate. And you will have many opportunities to learn each day. Another wonderful thing about Giraffe is that it only takes one person to use it—to defuse a conflict, to make a heartfelt connection, and to inspire co-operation.

Daily Practice

Notice your intention in communicating. Do you want to connect? Or do you want to be right or get your way?

Notice the flow of communication. Who is listening?

Check in with your feelings and needs throughout the day.

Practice observing what your children and others do and separating your observation from your evaluation.

Practice the respectful grammar of NVC: I feel because I need, you feel because you need, he feels because he needs.

Practice making concrete, present, do-able requests.

Cultivate your curiosity about what people are feeling and needing. Silently ask and answer: What could she be feeling right now? What are her needs?

Find more practical exercises for using NVC with kids in the booklet *Parenting from the Heart* by Inbal Kashtan (see Recommended Reading).

> The way of attentive love suggests listening to and talking with children—living with them instead of guiding their lives by remote control.
>
> —Nel Noddings

Key 6 ▪ Learn Together As You Go

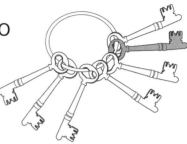

Key Concepts

- Whatever comes up, you can handle it.
- You and your kids can co-operate to make decisions and solve problems.
- There are lots of ways to meet needs.
- You can celebrate what works.
- You can learn from what doesn't work.

Have you found yourself finally getting a foothold in the issues and challenges of parenting an infant just when your darling baby outgrows midnight feedings, diapers, and midmorning naps and you're suddenly faced with the challenges of raising a toddler? Your hard-won, new skill-set for taking care of a baby has been outdated in only a few months. In a few months more, your toddler morphs into a four-year-old, and you're immersed in learning a new set of skills for a new set of challenges.

Each stage of your child's development, right up through adolescence (and beyond), requires you to learn new habits, create new structures, and develop new strategies to keep him or her learning, growing, and thriving. And it doesn't necessarily get easier the more children you have. Kids grow so fast that parents can't practice most of the new techniques they're learning long enough to master them, and the time between the toddlerhoods of the first- and second-born is long enough for parents to forget everything they thought they knew.

When kids are changing thoroughly and constantly, it's hard to feel confident that you're up to the challenge and that what you want to be passing along to them is being transmitted or received. To be successful

> **Everything is in a constant process of discovery and creating.**
>
> **Life is intent on finding what works, not what's "right."**
>
> —Margaret Wheatley

113

in handling such constant change with confidence rather than self-recrimination and doubt, (1) learn to learn as you go, and (2) co-operate with your kids to make decisions and solve problems.

▪ Whatever Comes Up, You Can Handle It

It is impossible for parents to plan for every stage of a child's development, to anticipate every change and be ready for it. So learning as you go not only makes sense, it seems to be required if you are going to keep pace with your child's growth. *Learning as you go* means you are learning to have faith that you can handle whatever comes up and to trust that things will work out. Learning as you go is based on the understanding that you are a learner about life in the same way that your kids are. It is supported by the realization that there are many ways to do things. It is based on the fact that we have a lot of choices, and if one way we've chosen to do something doesn't work, we are free to choose another and another. Learning as you go implies being awake, noticing little things, and being open and receptive rather than judgmental. Learning as you go encourages you to let go of rigid thoughts such as *there is only one right way* to do things, *people should* do certain things, or *somebody has to win and somebody has to lose*. Learning as you go is based, instead, on a belief that there are no failures—just new sets of circumstances to deal with.

▪ You and Your Kids Can Co-operate to Make Decisions and Solve Problems

Learning *together*, as you go, is based on the fact that you and your kids can be great partners for planning, decision making, and problem solving about things that affect their daily lives. Your kids are full of great ideas and love to share them. They are playful, fun, zany, open, interactive, outside-the-box thinkers. They want to contribute and to have a hand in deciding how their household operates. Learning together means that you trust that two heads are better than one because the outcome you get has the most potential to be satisfying for everyone.

One of the challenges of co-operating to solve problems is that it requires you to let go of the impulse to manage and control everything that affects your kids' lives. Letting go becomes easier when you realize that there are more strategies for solving problems than there are problems—more ways to meet needs than there are needs. When you co-investigate solutions, structures, and strategies with kids, your options and choices are limited only by your collective understanding of the situation at hand, your experiences, and your creative imaginations. It's a more playful and open-ended way to approach not just problems and concerns but every aspect of raising children. The spirit of it is, *Let's look at this situation together, see what everyone needs from it, and put our heads together to see how to address everyone's needs.* (Please remember that most of what kids ask for, such as video games, soda, or brand-name sneakers, are not needs but strategies for meeting needs. See Key 2 for more about needs and strategies.)

Co-investigating and co-creating with kids means taking risks and letting go of lots of *shoulds*. Your kids might suggest an idea for getting the dishes done: every member of the family washes his or her own plate, glass, and silverware, and two people rotate doing the pots and pans. It is a plan they are excited about; however, it doesn't match the way you think dishes should be done. Or what if your kids suggest sleeping in cotton sleeping bags (*because the sheets and blankets get too messy and are too big and difficult to straighten out every day*, they say) and this doesn't match your picture of what a bed should be. Are you willing to move outside of your comfort zone in order to experience the willing participation of your kids?

We encourage you to provide your kids with many opportunities to develop the confidence and skills to co-operate and find strategies that meet everyone's needs. To practice skills and build on successes, begin with some relatively simple activities that your family can decide on together:

planning how to spend the morning together

planning what order to do afternoon errands

> We never do anything wrong. We never have. We never will. We do things we wouldn't have done if we knew then what we are learning now.
>
> —Marshall B. Rosenberg

planning a meal

planning a party

celebrating a holiday

Explore for Yourself

In what areas do you and your children co-operate?

In what areas can you imagine more co-operation?

How do you feel when you imagine that level of co-operation?

▪ There Are Lots of Ways to Meet Needs

Meeting needs is the number one activity of life. Do you want this ongoing activity to be a chore or a pleasure? Whether fulfilling needs is a chore or a pleasure depends to a great extent on whether the world seems rich with an abundance of choices or bleak with a scarcity of them.

Whether it is apparent to you at this moment or not, most of you who are reading this book live in a world of abundance. For every need you have, there are many ways or strategies to fulfill it. Painting, sculpting, dancing, and singing are different ways to meet a need for creative expression. Reading, watching movies, listening to tapes, talking with others, or thinking quietly are ways to meet a need for learning. To meet needs for contributing to daily life at home, you can wash dishes, sweep the floor, prepare a meal, make a centerpiece for the table, or take out the trash. If it is fun you want, there are many ways to meet that need, as well.

Explore for Yourself

Select one need (from the Needs List in Key 5 or the Feelings & Needs Cards in Part III, Topic: Giraffe & Jackal Play) and identify several different ways you have found to satisfy that need. If you take the time to ponder these lists (or write them down), you may discover which ways have worked the best. You may also discover more ways you could try.

Explore Together: *Needs and Strategies*

Choose one of the needs from the Needs List or the Feelings & Needs Cards (referenced above) to explore together. List ways each person has found to meet that need. This can lead to a discussion of the effectiveness of these strategies. It can also lead to a discussion of new strategies to try. This activity often leads to increased awareness of the wealth of ways there are to meet needs.

If one way you try to meet a need doesn't work, you can try another. There are hundreds of opportunities each day to practice and refine your needs-meeting skills and to help your children refine theirs. With daily practice and plenty of patience—with yourself and with your children—you can continually create, invent, and intuit new ways to individually meet needs and to co-operate with others to meet needs together.

One mother we know had studied nutrition and valued providing healthy food for her family. She was a creative and skilled cook and enjoyed making meals for her husband and young son. Along with keeping healthy snacks in the house, she scheduled time each day to prepare a hot meal that would be served at six o'clock. She asked her husband and son to plan around it so they could eat together. However, when six o'clock arrived and dinner was on the table, her son was frequently absorbed in his own activities and didn't want to break his concentration for dinner. This was frustrating for a while. Then this mother realized that, as much as she enjoyed sitting down for dinner together, it wasn't the only way to feed her family healthy foods. She came up with another strategy, which was to stock a kitchen drawer with healthy snacks and a refrigerator drawer with carrots, celery, and apples. Her son was free to forage when he was too involved to come to meals.

Rather than arguing and fighting, use this step-by-step procedure to learn together with your children as you go:

> Feelings of worth can flourish only in an atmosphere where individual differences are appreciated, mistakes are tolerated, communication is open, and rules are flexible.
>
> —Virginia Satir

Steps for Learning Together As You Go

1. Identify the need or needs you or your child want to meet.

2. Choose a strategy for meeting the need.

3. Try out the strategy.

4. Evaluate the strategy: How well did it meet the needs that were identified?

5. Refine the strategy or try another one.

▪ You Can Celebrate What Works

When your strategies work and needs are met, take a few moments to acknowledge the success. It seems to be a human trait to focus on the negative, so it is important to take time to notice when things are going the way you want them to go. Feel your happiness, satisfaction, or delight. Taking time to celebrate successes anchors learning in your long-term memory and is a powerful way to build self-confidence.

Celebrating what works for your kids is another opportunity for empathic connection. Take time to listen for (1) the feelings they are having as a result of their accomplishments and (2) the needs they have met by doing what they have done. *Wow, you seem to be feeling very happy and proud of yourself for staying with that puzzle until you figured it out.*

When you keep the spotlight on your child's feelings and needs, you support her inner motivation to do things for her own reasons rather than to please others, gain rewards, or avoid punishment. You also teach her to evaluate for herself how well she is meeting her needs, rather than to look to others for evaluation.

True compassion is not just an emotional response but a firm commitment founded on reason.

—The Dalai Lama

Explore for Yourself

Think about a success you had today: something you did to meet a need that worked! What did you do?

What need did it meet?

Take a moment to celebrate. How do you feel knowing that it worked?

Explore Together: *Celebrate Successes*

Take turns sharing successes you've had this week.

■ You Can Learn from What Doesn't Work

When a strategy to fulfill a need doesn't work, it is tempting to say, *I made a mistake*, and spiral down into self-criticism, self-doubt, and self-punishment. In fact, a mistake is simply a strategy for meeting a need that didn't work out the way you hoped it would. Instead of playing a self-blame game and judging mistakes as bad, you can reconnect with your feelings and needs and tinker with, tweak, or otherwise adjust your strategies for more satisfying results.

If you are afraid of making mistakes, you will miss opportunities to try new things. You won't feel free to explore, experiment, and play. Rather than blame and judge yourself for making a mistake, learn from it and move on.

Steps for Learning from Mistakes

Observe: What did you do or say that you regret?

Notice: What are you telling yourself about what you did? Are you judging yourself?

Ask: What needs were you trying to meet?

Ask: How could you have met those needs more effectively?

Ask: Were there any needs you did meet?

Request: What do you want to do now to meet your needs?

Summary

No matter what you are faced with, you will be able to handle it if you are willing to be a learner along with your kids, co-investigating and co-creating as you go. Remember that there are many ways to do things and if one way doesn't work you can try another until you find a strategy that works for you. Celebrate what is working and learn from what isn't.

Only in growth,
reform, and
change,
paradoxically
enough,
is true security
to be found.

—Anne Morrow
    Lindbergh

Daily Practice

Notice when you feel anxious because you think something has to be done or something *should* be done in a particular way. Notice the judgment, breathe, and connect with the deeper need you want to meet. When you focus on the need, do other strategies come to mind that could meet that need?

Notice when you or your children are attached to a particular strategy. These phrases can give you a clue: *I have to do it, I need to have it, You need to do it.* See if you can sense the need or needs you or your kids want to meet through this strategy. See if there are other strategies that could also meet this need.

When something you do or your child does is successful in meeting a need, take a moment to celebrate.

When something you do or your child does is not successful, take time to feel the disappointment or sadness that may come up, then take yourself through the "Steps for Learning from Mistakes."

Key 7 ▪ Make Your Home a No-Fault Zone

Key Concepts

▪ Choose to see conflict as a problem to solve.
▪ Trust that your needs can get met.
▪ Trust that needs will lead to solutions.
▪ Co-operate to resolve conflicts.
▪ Move from the Battle Zone to the No-Fault Zone.

Keys 1 through 6 have been gradually showing you how to transform your home into a No-Fault Zone.

> These are the characteristics of a No-Fault Zone:
>
> Everyone attempts to understand the good reasons people do things.
>
> Everyone trusts that each person's needs will be considered and cared for.
>
> Everyone learns to focus on needs rather than on criticism or blame.
>
> Everyone co-operates to make life more fun and wonderful for one another.

Transforming your home into a No-Fault Zone has the potential to reduce conflict by 90 percent. To handle the other 10 percent that does come up, we share a way of seeing conflict that may be new to you. We also address the choices you have for handling heated interactions and give specific suggestions for working with these interactions co-operatively. We realize that growing the capacity to sustain fault-free interactions requires

Out beyond ideas of wrong-doing and right-doing, there is a field.

I'll meet you there.

—Rumi

121

practice and that there will be days when you are in the zone you want to be in and days when you aren't. For those off days and times, ideas are given for how to get back to your purpose for parenting and to your intention for co-operative interaction.

▪ Choose to See Conflict as a Problem to Solve

Conflict has gotten a bad rap. It is usually considered something to avoid, and parents often think that something's wrong with them or with their family when conflicts arise. Wherever people meet, however, there are going to be some clashes—some occasions when you bump into each other in the hallway of life. Learning together how to move around and with each other at these moments will serve you and your children well, now and for the rest of your life-long relationship.

The most common conflicts in homes everywhere have to do with ordinary, daily situations—bedtimes and rising times, sharing toys and household chores, what to buy at the store, and when and how to get out the door in the morning. These everyday occurrences don't have to become conflicts. With giraffe eyes and ears they can be viewed as puzzles or problems to solve and turned into discussions rather than arguments or fights. From this less emotional perspective, disagreements and clashes can be a chance for family members to reevaluate and explore their options as well as an opportunity for them to learn more about each other.

What stands in the way of seeing daily differences as problems to solve, rather than conflicts, is fear. Specifically, it is the fear that *I'm not going to be able to meet my needs.* This fear can quickly lead to anger (or other intense emotions), defensiveness, or aggression. When every member of the family trusts that his or her needs matter and will be addressed, the fear, tension, anger, and defensiveness surrounding everyday interactions begin to dissolve. Only then will you be able to welcome differences as problems to solve and opportunities to deepen family connections. The good news is, it takes only one person—one person practicing the skills developed in this book and trusting that by addressing everyone's needs differences can be worked out—to avert conflict. By developing your skills and holding this trust for your family, you can be the one to allay fears and prevent, reduce, and resolve conflict in your home.

The following story is an example of how a father averted conflict by focusing on his son's and his own needs rather than letting his fear turn to anger:

Dale, a dad who practices NVC, came home from work one day. Before he was through the door, his four-year-old son, Stevie, bounced up to greet him, grabbing hold of his pant leg and exclaiming, *Daddy, daddy, come play with me!* Immediately, Dale put his hand out to get some distance between them. Tension was apparent in his voice, *Not right now. Daddy's tired. I can play later.* Feeling this resistance, the boy started jumping up and down with insistence. Dale reacted in kind, repeating his message with increased firmness: *I said, Not right now. I'll play with you later.*

Then Dale stopped in his tracks. He noticed how uptight he was feeling and how sad, too, to feel and hear his negative response to Stevie's exuberance and eagerness to play with him. He knew he didn't want to continue on that track, so he took a couple of deep breaths and took a *Time In* to connect with his feelings and needs. *Hmmm. I'm feeling afraid. I see I'm worried I won't get a chance to wash up and unwind. I'm needing to protect myself, so I can shift my energy and relax. I really want to connect and play with Stevie.* Feeling more self-connected, Dale turned to his son with a proposal: *Hey, Stevie, I see you are really ready to play. And I'd like to play with you, too. I'd also like to change my clothes and wash up a bit. I have an idea. How about we sit on the couch for five minutes and you tell me all about your day. Then I'll go do the things I need to do before we play. What do you say?* Stevie responded, *How long will it take you, Dad?* And Dale replied, *I estimate fifteen minutes. Shall we time it?*

In some situations it may take more rounds of conversation than this to come up with a plan that everyone agrees to. However, Dale's ability

> To change something, build a new model that makes the existing model obsolete.
>
> —Buckminster Fuller

to get into a problem-solving conversation with Stevie rather than get into a conflict is what made all the difference here. When Dale noticed his fear that his need for relaxation wouldn't be met, he made a strategic choice: to stop going with the fear and instead take a *Time In* to check in with himself. He could then see that, along with relaxation, he also had a need to connect with Stevie. And he wanted to contribute to Stevie's needs for play and connection. Since Dale knew that there are ample strategies in the world to fulfill needs, it didn't take him long to shift his focus from protecting himself to proposing something that could work to meet both their needs.

When you don't see how you will meet all the needs present, you might feel perplexed, frustrated, or conflicted. However, it is when you also believe that you *can't* meet your needs that you will feel stronger feelings of fear, irritation, or desperation. Parents who know that there are abundant resources for solving problems find they can shift out of fear more quickly and relax when they don't know exactly how things will work out. When parents relax and trust that solutions are just around the corner, kids will relax, too, and trust that there are almost always satisfying solutions to be found.

▪ Trust That Your Needs Can Get Met

What makes it so difficult at times to trust that your needs can get met? If you have a backlog of experiences from the past in which your needs were not met, you may be inclined to doubt that they can or ever will be met. Trust will grow, however, when you take responsibility for your needs and take daily actions to fulfill them. As you develop more skills for meeting your own needs, fear, anger, defensiveness, and reactivity will subside.

Children also have fears about getting their needs met; their fears often lead to anger and defensiveness. Working with kids to recognize needs and find ways to meet them goes a long way to reduce anxiety and conflict.

With more confidence that your needs can be met and that you can

> The most destructive element in the human mind is fear. Fear creates aggressiveness.
>
> —Dorothy Thompson

help your kids meet their needs, you will be able to show your family a less reactive side of yourself; this experience has surprising benefits. You will be able to see beyond specific behaviors that scare and irritate you. You will have a better understanding of yourself and your kids. You will be steadier and calmer more of the time. Your kids might be doing the same things they have always done; however, your eyes and ears will now be seeing and hearing differently, allowing you to respond to their needs rather than react to their behavior.

Trusting that their needs matter to you, your kids will also relax and react less. They will not need to take a defensive stance and protect themselves from a parent who uses power-over tactics to get them to do things. And as this trust builds, you will experience a wonderful surprise —your kids will want to co-operate with you to meet your needs and find ways to live together that work for everyone.

▪ Trust That Needs Will Lead to Solutions

Remember, there is an abundant universe full of strategies to meet needs. Conflict occurs when you and your child, or any two or more people, lose sight of this fact. Feelings of impatience, anxiety, or fear may come up until you have a solution in sight, or until you regain trust that a solution will come.

As we understand it, conflict occurs when a need is urgently calling, you don't see how you can meet this need in the situation, *and* you fear that it can't get met.

A common conflict in families comes up when one family member wants to relax by increasing the volume on the CD player and another family member wants to relax in quiet. Conflicts happen when children want to play together but one wants to play on the swings and the other wants to play cards. Conflicts happen when one family member wants to celebrate a family holiday by going out and another family member wants to celebrate at home. Quite frequently, as in these examples, you will see that the needs involved are the same for both parties—in these examples, the needs are for relaxation, play, and celebration.

While it is not always the case that the needs are the same, it *is* always the case that it is the strategies that are in conflict, not the needs. As you come to trust in an abundant universe and to see a range of possibilities for meeting needs, you will find that you don't hold on so fearfully to your favorite strategies.

▪ Co-operate to Resolve Conflicts

At times when you do feel fearful or feel any other heightened emotions, choosing to connect and co-operate with your child may be the farthest thing from your mind. Indeed, you might at those times experience the "emotional hijacking" mentioned in Chapter 2. Heightened emotions swamp your thinking; your more reasoned brain functioning is diminished, leaving you with charged feelings; you feel the urge to charge ahead with what you think you need; and you forget that you have any choices other than to follow that urge. We'd like to review here the choices you do have in any and all situations. You may want to post this list somewhere to remind yourself of these choices at moments of emotional hijacking.

Peace cannot be kept by force. It can only be achieved by understanding.

—Albert Einstein

Three Choices for Moments of Conflict

1. *You can decide you want to be right and get your way no matter what.*

This choice most often leads to using power-over tactics to get what you want (tactics such as angry outbursts, arguments, fighting, sulking, or walking away and refusing to talk). These actions are very likely to escalate conflict in the moment and in the future.

2. *You can ignore it and hope it goes away.*

When your discomfort around conflict gets the better of you or you don't see a way to deal with it that won't make it worse, there's a temptation to walk away and hope it disappears. Sometimes things do sort themselves out and you're off the hook. More often than not, however, the conflict doesn't go away and the same old battle comes back, but bigger, more complicated, and more difficult to sort out than ever.

3. *You can hold the intention to connect and co-operate.*

When your intention is to connect and co-operate, you seek to understand everyone's needs in the situation and you hold all needs equally. You will work with others to find the best solution you can to meet mutual needs—a solution that everyone can feel good about.

Neither of the first two options give the results parents want, and yet these are the choices parents make every day, by default, when they are unaware of or ignore their third option.

▪ Move from the Battle Zone to the No-Fault Zone

When you find yourself emotionally charged and in the battle zone with your child (or anyone else)—when you notice that you are feeling upset, afraid, or angry, and doing things such as raising your voice, arguing, name-calling, or blaming—we hope you will remember that there is another place you could be, a fault-free place that would be much more productive and satisfying for everyone. Just remembering that such a place exists can help you change direction.

To get to that different, calmer place, follow these steps: (1) First, Hit the Pause Button and stop doing anything you will regret later. (2) Next, do what you need to do to Regain Equilibrium: take some deep breaths, go for a walk or a run, do yoga, or get empathy from a friend. (3) Then, Connect with Your Feelings and Needs as soon as possible. If you are angry, take the time to identify the anger-producing thoughts that are the source and fuel for anger. Feel the feelings and sit with the needs that are urgently calling for your attention. (4) Finally, Reconnect with Your Intention and Purpose, the one you established in Key 1 for how you want to interact with your children. Make your next move from *that* place.

You can help your children redirect their energy when they are charged up or spinning out of control by coaching them through these same moves. At noncharged moments, or during family meetings, you can go over the steps and explore activities that restore you so you and your kids can operate from choice more of the time. (For activities to calm yourself and transform anger, see "D-Stress," "Re-charge," and "Transform Anger" in Part III, Topic: Life-Enriching Practices.)

When emotions are highly charged, it makes good sense to delay conversation about conflict until attention, mental focus, and goodwill have returned. Once everyone is calm and enjoying themselves again, however, these conversations are often forgotten or put off indefinitely. No one wants to talk about conflict and risk spoiling the good time. As a consequence, the issues often don't get addressed at all, and they usually resurface later in a new and often intensified conflict. If you do choose to put off discussion about a conflict, remember to take it up later, during a time of ease and sweet connection, when it can be most productive.

If a simple conversation doesn't take you to the connection you want, and a conflict arises, there are two powerful processes explained in Part III that will help everyone be heard and help guide everyone back to mutual understanding and respect. One activity can be done alone: "Resolve Your Own Conflict." The other involves a third party who facilitates a "Giraffe Mediation." These and other activities for peaceful conflict resolution can be found in the activities list at the front of Part III or in the list of Charts and Activities at the front of the book.

Summary

Build a No-Fault Zone and they will come.

If you can envision a place where respect and co-operation reign, you are on your way to creating it. If you have a deep longing for connection and harmony, you are on the way to bringing it into being. Once you choose these as your purposes and intentions for creating a home, you can, one step at a time, one day at a time, align your thoughts and actions to create it. The 7 keys in this book, with the exercises and activities, can unlock this creative capacity in you. We call the place where respect and co-operation reign the No-Fault Zone. You might want to choose a different name.

Although attempting to bring about world peace through the internal transformation of individuals is difficult, it is the only way.

—The Dalai Lama

In this place, everyone attempts to understand the good reasons people do things. You and your children trust that your needs will be considered and cared for. A respectful focus on needs replaces criticism, blame, and punishment. And everyone co-operates to make life more fun and wonderful for one another.

The thirteenth-century Persian philosopher-poet Rumi describes this place as a field out beyond wrong-doing and right-doing. If you create such a fault-free place, whether it is a field or a castle, others will want to join you there because they too are longing for it in their hearts. Your home will be a place your kids want to be. And, each parent who creates a home based on mutual respect and co-operation moves us all closer to creating a peaceful and sustainable world.

PART III

Family Activities & Stories from the No-Fault Zone

Part III provides a wide range of games, activities, and stories for fun, inspiration, and additional skill development. To locate individual activities by name or by topic, see the activities list located at the beginning of Part III or the list of Charts and Activities at the front of the book.

Family Activities

Topic: Giraffe & Jackal Culture

Title: Introduction to Giraffe Language & Jackal Language

In all cultures, language sustains certain ways of seeing, thinking, expressing, and listening. Giraffe Language expresses and supports a culture that values honesty, compassion, and respectful interactions. It demonstrates the love that is promoted by spiritual traditions around the world.

For thousands of years, however, people have been learning and using language that makes respectful, co-operative relationships difficult. This language has contributed to a tremendous amount of pain in the world, including conflicts that arise every day in families.

Jackal Language

The Jackal is the symbol of this habitual language because jackals run low to the ground and have a limited view of things. When thinking and speaking in Jackal Language, a person sees a very limited range of choices about how to do things:

labels people: *You're mean. She's bossy. He's dumb. I'm lazy.*

judges: *I'm right. You're wrong. We're good. They're bad.*

blames: *It's her fault. You should have. I'm to blame.*

denies choice: *You have to. You can't. I can't. They made me.*

makes demands: *If you don't do what I say, you'll be sorry.*

Far from facilitating heartfelt connections and co-operation, Jackal Language serves to disconnect people from themselves and one another. Yet with no other models for a different way of speaking, it is taken for granted.

Giraffe Language[1]

The language of compassion goes by many names: Nonviolent Communication (NVC), Compassionate Communication, and the Language of Life. It is also known as Giraffe Language because giraffes have the largest heart of any land animal and because the giraffe's neck gives it a long and broad perspective on life.

A Giraffe perspective includes vision and a big heart—an integration of thinking and feeling. People speaking Giraffe Language can see many ways to meet needs, and they stick their necks out to be honest about what's going on for them, to ask for what they want, and to listen to what others feel and need.

Many teachers of NVC use Giraffe and Jackal puppets and ears to clarify key distinctions.[2] The puppets and ears also provide visual cues for role-plays and contribute fun and laughter to the learning process. Puppets and ears are not necessary for learning NVC; however, most young children and adults enjoy them. Young people between the ages of ten and eighteen years old often view puppets and ears as childish.

Giraffe and Jackal metaphors are meant to be convenient and fun terms referring to two kinds of thinking, not labels to support a belief that there are two kinds of people. We are all susceptible to Jackal thinking, listening, and talking. And anyone can begin now to learn Giraffe, a language of compassion and respect.

---

1. The International Center for Nonviolent Communication's use of the image and term Giraffe is in no way connected to The Giraffe Project, a completely separate organization that has its own training and educational materials.

2. Puppets and ears can be purchased at the website for the Center for Nonviolent Communication, www.cnvc.org. Some of the activities in this book make use of Giraffe and Jackal Ears, so we have included a template for making your own. (See "Giraffe & Jackal Ears" in Topic: Giraffe & Jackal Play.)

What Language Are You Using?

☐ **Giraffe Language**	☐ **Jackal Language**
Acknowledges Choice	**Denies Choice**
I choose to, I want to, I can.	I have to, I must.
There are many ways to meet needs.	I can't.
	There's only one way.
Perceives Abundance	**Perceives Scarcity**
There's enough if we share.	There's not enough to go around.
Everyone's needs can be met.	We can't meet everyone's needs.
It's you and me.	It's you or me.
Observes and Expresses	**Evaluates and Judges**
I see, I hear, I remember . . .	Here's what happened . . .
	You're too . . .
	He's mean; she's rude.
Takes Responsibility for My Own Feelings and Needs	**Blames Others/ Blames Self**
I feel . . . *because I need* . . .	I feel . . . *because you* . . .
Asks for What I Would Like	**Makes Demands**
Here's what I'd like.	You have to . . .
If you're willing.	If you don't . . .
Listens Empathically	**Listens Selectively**
Are you feeling . . . ? because you need . . . ?	Suggests, lectures, advises, argues, fixes, analyzes

What Language Do You Want to Use?

Topic: Family Meetings

Title: Co-Create Agreements

Objective: To make and work with family agreements
that meet needs for everyone

Type of Activity: Introduction

When everyone who is affected by agreements also participates in making them, several things happen that contribute to respect and co-operation. Everyone becomes an active participant in family decision-making. And co-creating family agreements generally meets needs for participation, respect, consideration, and assurance that needs matter in the home, for parents as well as for kids.

In contrast, when parents set the rules and determine the consequences for breaking them, parents become the enforcers who note when transgressions occur and hand out punishments.

To co-create family agreements, begin by asking the question: *What kind of home do you want? What do you need to feel safe enough to be yourself?*

Needs most often expressed are safety, learning, respect, consideration for others, and care for the environment. Once a list of needs is generated, each family member can list some behaviors that would help meet those needs.

So what happens when someone in the family does something that doesn't meet the needs expressed by the other family members?

Any family member can (1) express what s/he observes, (2) express how s/he feels about what is going on, (3) say what needs s/he has that are not met by what is happening, and (4) make a very specific request.

The primary point to be made here is that no one steps in to punish a wrongdoer. Those people who are affected when another family member doesn't observe the agreements need to speak for themselves and ask for what they want.

Topic: Family Meetings

Title: Create a Mission Statement

Objective: To create a family statement of how you want to interact with one another and what is individually and collectively important to you (this is a good way to establish a sense of safety, trust, and belonging)

Type of Activity: Discussing and writing

Materials: White or colored paper, colored markers and/or colored pencils

Procedure: Each person contributes ideas about what she or he needs to feel physically and emotionally safe. Compile the ideas into one statement. See the following examples:

Example 1:

> *We want to make our home a place that is safe for everyone—*
> *A place where we are allowed to feel what we feel, to need what we*
>   *need, and to ask for what we want to meet our needs,*
> *A place where we can be honest and say the truth as we each see it,*
> *A place where there is no criticizing, blaming, or shaming*
> *A place where the needs of each of us are seen as equally important,*
>   *and where*
> *We all work together to meet the most needs possible.*

Example 2:

> *This is a Safe Place.*
> *We laugh, we learn, & we grow, together.*

Your statement can be decorated, framed, and hung where everyone can see it as a reminder of what you have all decided you want your home to be. It serves as your mutual vision for the family you want to create. You can work together to bring your daily practices into alignment with your family statement.

Topic: Family Meetings

Title: Family Empathy Check-In[1]

Objective: To connect with your feelings and needs, and with family members

Type of Activity: Interactive

Materials: Feelings and Needs Cards (find them in Topic: Giraffe & Jackal Play) (optional: a Feelings List and a Needs List to refer to and to make extra cards)

Procedure:

1. Sit around a table or in a circle on the floor. Spread all of the **Needs** Cards, face up, in the space between you, so everyone can see them.

2. One person (the Speaker) holds all of the **Feelings** Cards. The Speaker tells a short story about something that happened recently and chooses the **Feelings** Cards that represent his or her feelings in the situation, then puts these cards, face up, in front of him or her.

3. The person to the left of the Speaker makes an empathic guess by picking up one **Needs** Card, placing it in front of the Speaker, and asking the Speaker: *I wonder if you feel/felt* (reflect one or more of the **Feelings** that the Speaker mentioned) *because you need/needed* (state the need on the selected **Needs** Card)*?*

The Speaker does not respond to this or any of the subsequent guesses until all guesses are made. The Speaker simply receives empathic guesses and reflects on the needs that are offered.

4. Continuing around the circle, one person at a time takes a turn making an empathic guess and putting before the Speaker one **Needs** Card.

---

1. This activity is based on *Empathy Poker*, developed by Lucy Leu.

When a player senses that the relevant needs have been guessed and there are no more **Needs** Cards on the floor that they want to guess, the player may say, *I pass.*

5. When all guesses have been made, the Speaker says which needs hit home the most. At this point, the Speaker can also select any **Needs** Cards that weren't guessed that are important in the situation. Then, all **Needs** Cards go back in the center and the **Feelings** Cards are passed to the player on the left, who becomes the new Speaker.

Variation: *Wild Cards*

Jokers/wild cards can be used to guess any additional feelings and needs that are not already in the deck.

Variation: *Show of Cards*

For a quick family check-in, each family member starts with a deck of Feelings & Needs Cards. At the beginning of Family Meetings, or anytime someone calls for a "Show of Cards," each person can hold up for others to see, the Feelings Card(s) and Needs Card(s) that express what's going on for them.

Topic: Family Meetings

Title: Is That an Observation?

Objective: To distinguish between observations and evaluations

Type of Activity: Reading, writing, sorting, discussing, game playing

Materials: 3 different colors of construction paper, felt pen, Statement Strips (see following page)

Preparation:

- Observation: A statement that is free from judgment or evaluation of any kind. To make an observation, pretend you are looking through the lens of a video camera, then describe the sights and sounds the camera would record. An example of an observation is, *I see you looking in your book while I'm talking to you.*

- Evaluation: A statement that contains your beliefs, thoughts, and opinions about what you are seeing or hearing. An example of an evaluation is, *You never listen to me.*

Procedure:

1. Review the difference between observations and evaluations.

2. Cut out the Statement Strips, fold them in half, and place them in a bowl.

3. Write headings on the construction paper: OBSERVATION, EVALUATION, and "?" (for statements you are uncertain about) and place the papers in the center of a table.

4. One at a time, each person at the table draws a folded strip of paper, decides whether it is an observation, evaluation, or whether she or he is uncertain, and then places it on the appropriate piece of construction paper.

5. Continue taking turns until all the strips have been placed on one of the three pieces of paper.

6. Then, discuss and decide together where to place strips placed on the piece of construction paper marked "?".

7. When all strips have been placed on the Observation or the Evaluation papers, read all of the Observations to see if any Evaluations have been mixed in. Also, read all of the Evaluations to see if any Observations have been mixed in with them.

Statement Strips for "Is That an Observation?"

She gave me a cookie.	She is generous.
I ended up bleeding the last time we played together.	You play too rough.
He asked me to join the game.	He is really friendly.
They are pressing their noses against the window.	They're acting stupid.
She burped.	That's rude.
You finished all your dinner.	You are such a good eater.
You are sitting with your legs stretched out.	You are taking up too much room.
She put mustard on her apple.	That's gross.
He read two books this week.	He's smart.
You sat on my glasses. Now they are crooked.	You stupid idiot!
You bumped into me.	You are so clumsy.
He pushed me out of line.	He's a bully.
You stayed inside after I asked you to come out.	You are a poor sport.
You ate the last two pieces of pie.	You are a selfish pig.
She said I couldn't join the game.	That's mean.
He told the teacher that I took his pencil.	He's a tattle tale.
She came to see me when I was sick.	She is a good friend.
I spent two hours doing homework.	You are such a good student.
There's glue on the table.	You always make such a mess.

Topic: Family Meetings

Title: Needs List

Objective: To understand needs, develop a needs vocabulary, & have a common list of needs to refer to

Type of Activity: Discussing and writing

Materials: Large piece of white paper or posterboard, colored markers and/or colored pencils

Procedure:

1. Discuss the things that everyone in the world needs and write them on the paper or posterboard.

2. Illustrate the needs where possible.

3. Make a decorative border and put it on the refrigerator door.

Topic: Family Meetings

Title: Needs Mandala

Objective: To develop a vocabulary and appreciation of needs

Type of Activity: Art and writing

Materials: Large piece of cardboard, old magazines with lots of pictures, glue, ribbon

Procedure:

1. Cut a large circle from a piece of cardboard.

2. Draw lines to divide the circle into six parts. (The divisions don't need to be pie shapes.)

3. Write one of the following in each area: Survival needs (food, water, shelter), Safety/Protection, Belonging/Acceptance, Learning/Respect, Choice/Self-Direction, Community.

4. Cut out pictures from magazines to represent these needs and glue them on the circle.

5. When all of the cardboard is covered, glue a piece of ribbon or piping around the edge of the circle to frame it, and then hang it on a wall. If you want to make it into a mobile, decorate both sides and hang it from the ceiling.

Topic: Family Meetings

Title: Needs Treasure Chest

Objective: To develop a vocabulary of needs; to honor the preciousness of needs

Type of Activity: Art and writing

Materials: Colored paper cut into jewel shapes (circles, diamonds, hearts, squares, rectangles, etc.), envelopes

Procedure:

1. Ask everyone what is important to each of them (what they value) in relationships with friends, in themselves, in family members, in nature, in school, at home, etc.

2. Suggest that needs are like precious jewels.

3. Write what you value on the paper jewels.

4. Decorate the envelopes to be the treasure chests for the jewels.

5. Share your jewels with one another.

6. Notice common needs and values that everyone agrees are important.

Topic: Family Meetings

Title: Fortune Cookies

Objective: To learn to distinguish between observations and evaluations

Type of Activity: Co-operative game

Materials: A plate of fortune cookies, enough for 4–5 cookies for each family member; a set of 4 cards for each person (3 x 5 inch index cards work well). On the first card, write a large F or the word Fortune; on the second card, make a large E or Evaluation; on the third card, write a large O or Observation; on the last card, write a ? (question mark).

Preparation:

Discuss the distinctions between:

A Fortune: a statement that something will happen in the future

You will have good luck tomorrow.

An Evaluation: a statement pretending to know what a person is

You are a happy person.

An Observation: something that a video camera could see or a tape recorder could record

The cat is sitting in your lap purring.

Procedure:

This is a dessert game so you could make a pot of tea to go with the cookies.

The idea is to have fun while exploring together the difference between a fortune, an evaluation, and an observation by reading from the slips of paper in fortune cookies.

Take turns picking out a fortune cookie, opening it, and reading the fortune. (And eating it if you want.) Everyone then holds up a card to indicate they don't know or they think the statement is a Fortune, an Evaluation, or an Observation. Continue as long as everyone's having fun.

Variation: Paper Cookies

Make your own paper fortune cookies by cutting out 3- or 4-inch-round pieces of tan paper. Fold each piece twice to resemble the shape of a fortune cookie. Open up the "cookies" and whoever wants to writes a statement inside that could be a fortune, an observation, an evaluation, or something else. Then fold the cookies and place them in a bowl. One at a time, select a cookie, read it, and discuss what type of statement it is.

Topic: Family Meetings

Title: Feelings Books

Objective: To explore feelings; to see that all feelings are okay; to build a feelings vocabulary

Type of Activity: Writing and drawing

Materials: Construction paper for the book pages, colored pencils, markers (optional: magazines for cutting out pictures, scissors, glue, decorative paper for book covers)

Procedure:

Individual Feelings Books:

Each family member makes a book out of construction paper. Write a separate feeling word on each page and draw, color, and/or cut out pictures in magazines to convey how you experience this feeling.

Family Feelings Books:

Make a Family Feelings Book for each feeling you'd like to explore together. You could title them *I Feel Curious*, *I Feel Joyful*, *I Feel Sad*, *I Feel Afraid*, *I Feel Peaceful*. Each family member fills out one or more pages by drawing and/or writing about that feeling.

Topic: Family Meetings

Title: Feelings Leaves

Objective: To see the connection between feelings and needs (feelings arise from our met and unmet needs)

Type of Activity: Art

Materials: Large chart paper, several 6-inch squares of green paper, crayons, markers, tape

Preparation:

Introduce the concept of universal needs and create a Needs List prior to this activity. (For samples of needs lists, see Keys 2 & 5 and the activity "Needs List" in Topic: Family Meetings.)

Familiarize yourself with the connection between Feelings and Needs. (See Keys 2 & 5.)

Procedure:

1. On the chart paper, someone draws two large trees without leaves. One tree has upturned branches and the title: When Needs Are Met. The other tree has downturned branches with the title: When Needs Are Not Met.

2. Explore where feelings come from, suggesting that all of our feelings come from our needs. Some feelings arise when our needs are met. Explore: What feelings do you have when your need for hunger is met? For play? For learning something new? Some other feelings arise when our needs are not met. Explore: What feelings do you have when your need for rest is not met? For understanding? For friends?

3. Make Feeling Leaves by folding squares of green paper in half and tearing them in the shape of a half leaf, then unfolding the paper to reveal a leaf. You can also use scissors to cut leaf shapes. Copy feelings words from the Feelings List in Key 5 onto the leaves, one feeling word per leaf.

4. Spread the leaves on a table or on the floor. Place them so the feeling word is showing. Then, one at a time, pick up a leaf, say the feeling word, and decide if you feel this feeling when your need is met or when it is not met. Then tape the feeling leaf to the tree you think it belongs to. (Note: Most feeling words are clearly associated with met or unmet needs. Some feeling words, like "surprise" could go on either tree.)

Topic: Family Meetings

Title: Chain of Gift Giving

Objective: To appreciate the many gifts family members
have to give

Type of Activity: Interactive

Materials: Typing paper, strips of construction paper
(1 x 9 inches) in many colors, glue, tape, or stapler

Procedure:

1. Have each member of the family put his or her name at the top of a piece of paper and make a list of the gifts they have to give. Other members of the family can contribute to what goes on the list.

2. Cut construction paper into strips about 1 inch by 9 inches.

3. Each family member then copies each gift from their list to a colored strip of paper.

4. Assemble a chain of gifts family members have to give and tack it around a doorway or place it in some other agreed-upon place.

5. Keep adding to the chain.

Topic: Life-Enriching Practices

Title: Give Gratitude

Objective: To nurture your compassionate heart; to develop a practice that supports choice and respectful interactions

Type of Activity: Family discussion, family journaling, individual journaling

Materials: One notebook for a Family Gratitude Journal or individual notebooks

Procedure:

1. Discuss the meaning and feeling of gratitude. Use the following quotes for inspiration:

   Gratitude is the memory of the heart.　　　　—French proverb

   The more you practice the art of thankfulness, the more you have to be thankful for. This, of course, is a fact. Thankfulness does tend to reproduce in kind. The attitude of gratitude revitalizes the entire mental process by activating all other attitudes, thus stimulating creativity.
   　　　　　　　　　　　　　　　　　　　—Norman Vincent Peale

2. Take turns giving one answer to the question: *For what are you grateful?*

3. Make a Family Gratitude Journal, where family members can add one gratitude per page, writing or drawing about what it is they are grateful for.

4. Individuals can make their own Gratitude Journal to fill in at the end of the day. You can use purchased notebooks with lined or blank pages or you can make your own book. You can also create Gratitude Journal pages with a form similar to this:

   Date:
   My need for _____ was met today when _____.

Topic: Life-Enriching Practices

Title: D-Stress[1]

Objective: To synchronize the rhythms of the breath, mind, and heart

Type of Activity: Inner awareness

Procedure:

1. **Notice that you are feeling stressed.**

2. **Hit the pause button.**
   Immediately stop what you are doing. You are about to do something you are likely to regret later. If you do not push the pause button your upset is likely to increase.

3. **Focus on your heart and breath.**
   Breathe into the area of the heart (4 counts)
   Exhale through the abdomen (4 counts)

4. **Create a feeling of gratitude or appreciation.**
   Remember a time when you were feeling these feelings and feel them again now.

5. **Breathe another 6 or 8 breaths while holding that feeling.**

6. **Check in.**
   Ask yourself: *Am I feeling any differently?*
   Are any new ideas for handling the problem coming to mind?

---

1. Adapted from a HeartMath Freeze-Frame Exercise in *The Inside Story: Understanding the Power of Feelings*, HeartMath L.L.C., 2002.

Topic: Life-Enriching Practices

Title: Re-Charge

Objective: To provide choices for deep rest and relaxation

Type of Activity: Inner awareness

Procedure:

When you run out of patience and energy, it is time to Re-Charge—to restore yourself to your healthiest, most balanced state. Without consciously taking time to do it, it won't happen.

Ask yourself these questions:

When do I feel happiest?

What activities give me joy and well-being?

With what person or people do I feel most myself?

In what places do I feel most peaceful and calm?

Include these places, people, and activities in your life as often as possible.

Topic: Life-Enriching Practices

Title: Take *Time In*

Objective: To calm yourself when you are feeling stress, anger, or other heightened, negative emotions; to connect with your feelings and needs

Type of Activity: Inner awareness

Procedure:

1. Notice your symptoms.

You are feeling stressed or in a heightened emotional state.

Physical symptoms:
These can be different for different people. Some of these symptoms might include: increased heart rate; clammy or sweaty hands; feeling warmer than usual, especially around the neck and in the face; and tightness in the chest or throat.

Action symptoms:
Speaking in a louder than usual voice; name-calling; using put downs; threatening yourself or others; and/or pushing, slapping, shaking, hitting, or spanking another person.

2. Hit the pause button.

Immediately stop what you are doing. You are about to do something you are likely to regret later. If you do not push the pause button your upset is likely to increase.

3. Regain equilibrium.

Take several deep breaths.

Go for a walk or run.

Do some stretches.

Call a friend for empathy.

4. Connect with feelings and needs.

As soon as possible, connect with your feelings and needs.

If you are angry, identify the anger-producing thoughts that fuel the anger.

Feel the feelings and sit with the needs that are urgently calling for your attention.

Option: *Empathy Solitaire*

You can use the Feelings and Needs card deck at the end of the book to help you determine feelings and needs. Look through the Feelings Cards and lay out the cards that describe your feelings. Look through the Needs Cards and lay out the cards that describe the unmet needs that you think might be behind your feelings.

5. Reconnect with your Purpose and your Intention for communication.

6. Make your next move from this place of connection with yourself, your purpose, and your intention.

Topic: Life-Enriching Practices

Title: Assess Your Needs (for Parents)

Objective: To stay current with life; to celebrate met needs and mourn unmet needs; to notice needs that want attention

Type of Activity: Self-assessment for parents

Procedure:

Make copies of this form so you can write on it and periodically review and assess your needs. Circle the number that represents your current level of satisfaction or dissatisfaction in meeting the following needs (5 indicating most satisfaction, 1 indicating most dissatisfaction).

My Relationship with Myself

1—2—3—4—5	nutrition
1—2—3—4—5	rest
1—2—3—4—5	exercise
1—2—3—4—5	fun
1—2—3—4—5	balance
1—2—3—4—5	self-expression
1—2—3—4—5	creative outlets
1—2—3—4—5	meaning, spiritual connection
1—2—3—4—5	learning, growth
1—2—3—4—5	contribution
1—2—3—4—5	companionship

My Relationship with My Children

1—2—3—4—5	safety & trust
1—2—3—4—5	mutual respect
1—2—3—4—5	co-operation
1—2—3—4—5	expressing my feelings & needs clearly
1—2—3—4—5	hearing their feelings & needs
1—2—3—4—5	hearing the needs behind their *No*
1—2—3—4—5	asking for what I would like without making demands
1—2—3—4—5	having fun together

My Relationship with Other Adults at Home

1—2—3—4—5	safety & trust
1—2—3—4—5	co-operation
1—2—3—4—5	expressing my feelings & needs clearly
1—2—3—4—5	hearing their feelings & needs
1—2—3—4—5	hearing requests, not demands
1—2—3—4—5	asking for what I would like without making demands
1—2—3—4—5	having fun together

Topic: Life-Enriching Practices

Title: Assess Your Needs (for Kids)

Objective: To know what's going on with you; to meet your needs better

Type of Activity: Self-assessment for kids

Procedure:

Make copies of this form so you can write on it and periodically review and assess your needs. Circle the number that shows how satisfied you are with meeting your needs (5 = most satisfied, 1 = not satisfied).

My Relationship with Myself

1—2—3—4—5	I eat healthy foods
1—2—3—4—5	I get rest
1—2—3—4—5	I get exercise
1—2—3—4—5	I have fun
1—2—3—4—5	I know how to calm myself when angry or upset
1—2—3—4—5	I have fun creating
1—2—3—4—5	I know why I do things
1—2—3—4—5	I enjoy learning
1—2—3—4—5	I have friends
1—2—3—4—5	I like myself

My Relationship with My Parents

1—2—3—4—5　　I feel safe

1—2—3—4—5　　I know they care about me

1—2—3—4—5　　I tell them what I feel & need

1—2—3—4—5　　I hear what they feel & need

1—2—3—4—5　　I ask for what I want without
making demands

1—2—3—4—5　　They ask for what they want
without making demands

1—2—3—4—5　　We have fun together

1—2—3—4—5　　We make decisions together

My Relationship with My Brothers & Sisters

1—2—3—4—5　　I feel safe

1—2—3—4—5　　We care about each other

1—2—3—4—5　　We know how to work things out
together

1—2—3—4—5　　I express my feelings & needs &
what I want

1—2—3—4—5　　I hear their feelings & needs & what
they want

1—2—3—4—5　　We have fun together

Topic: Life-Enriching Practices

Title: Giraffe Notes of Appreciation

Objective: To develop skills in composing, writing, and delivering a Giraffe appreciation

Type of Activity: Writing

Materials: Giraffe Note forms (see following page)

Preparation: Familiarity with observations, feelings, needs, and requests

Procedure:

1. Introduce the Giraffe Notes at a family meeting by asking everyone to think of something that another family member did that met a need for him or her.

2. Demonstrate filling out the Giraffe Note expressing appreciation.

3. Have each family member write a Giraffe Note and deliver it.

4. Everyone can share how they feel after writing the note as well as what needs were met by doing the activity. They can also share how it feels to receive a note and what needs are met by receiving appreciation.

5. The notes can be colored and decorated.

Note: Children who aren't yet writing can draw a picture that shows appreciation. The picture can be about the event or about how they felt when the family member met his or her need.

Keep a stack of Giraffe Notes in a place where everyone can get to them easily. Encourage everyone to fill out at least one a day. They are fun surprises at the dinner table or shared at family meetings. Eventually your children may start to share Giraffe Notes with other relatives, teachers, and friends at school.

Giraffe Note of Appreciation

When I think about . . . .

I feel . . . .

Because it meets my need for . . . .

Topic: Life-Enriching Practices

Title: Giraffe Journal

Objective: To learn and practice self-empathy for situations that didn't go the way you wanted; to get in the habit of celebrating situations that did go as you wanted

Type of Activity: Writing

Materials: Giraffe Journal forms (see below)

Preparation: Familiarity with observations, feelings, needs, and requests

Procedure:

Use this form to journal about a situation. Write down your observations of the situation, your feelings, your needs, and any requests you have of yourself or someone else.

You can use this form for giving yourself self-empathy, working through a situation that didn't go the way you wanted, celebrating, and/or expressing gratitude. You can photocopy the form from the book, or make your own version.

Giraffe Journal ▪ *Giraffe Journal* ▪ *Giraffe Journal* ▪ *Giraffe Journal*

DATE:

The situation/observations:

My feelings:

My needs:

Requests of myself or others:

Giraffe Journal ▪ *Giraffe Journal* ▪ *Giraffe Journal* ▪ *Giraffe Journal*

DATE:

The situation/observations:

My feelings:

My needs:

Requests of myself or others:

Giraffe Journal ▪ *Giraffe Journal* ▪ *Giraffe Journal* ▪ *Giraffe Journal*

DATE:

The situation/observations:

My feelings:

My needs:

Requests of myself or others:

Giraffe Journal ▪ *Giraffe Journal* ▪ *Giraffe Journal* ▪ *Giraffe Journal*

DATE:

The situation/observations:

My feelings:

My needs:

Requests of myself or others:

Topic: Life-Enriching Practices

Title: Translate Judgments into Needs Messages

Objective: To learn to translate judgments into needs messages

Type of Activity: Self-reflective exercise

Materials: Paper (or copies of the forms below) and pen or pencil

Preparation: A judgment is a tragic expression of needs. It doesn't express clearly what the person is feeling and needing, and it most often triggers more judgment and blame. When you learn to hear the needs message behind the judgment, you will increase understanding, connection, choice, and peace.

Judgments your child (or someone else) makes of you.

Example: Your child says: *You never listen to me.*

Your feelings and needs: *I feel sad. I need to be understood and to contribute.*

Guess your child's feelings and needs: *She feels hurt. She needs to matter and be heard.*

Your child says: _____

Your feelings and needs: _____

Guess your child's feelings and needs: _____

Your child says: _____

Your feelings and needs: _____

Guess your child's feelings and needs: _____

Your child says: _____

Your feelings and needs: _____

Guess your child's feelings and needs: _____

Your child says: _____

Your feelings and needs: _____

Guess your child's feelings and needs: _____

Judgments you make about your child (or someone else).

Example: Your judgment: *She's a motor mouth.*

Your feelings and needs: *I'm irritated because I want consideration and choice.*

Your judgment: _____

Your feelings and needs: I feel _____ because I need _____

Your judgment: _____

Your feelings and needs: I feel _____ because I need _____

Your judgment: _____

Your feelings and needs: I feel _____ because I need _____

Your judgment: _____

Your feelings and needs: I feel _____ because I need _____

Topic: Life-Enriching Practices

Title: Transform Anger into a Life-Enriching Message

Objective: To learn to transform anger into feelings and needs

Type of Activity: Self-reflective exercise

Materials: None required (optional: paper and pen or pencil)

Preparation: There are two things to understand about anger:

- Anger is a red flag alerting you that an important need is not being met.

- The goal is not to deny or judge anger, rather, to defuse the charge so you can hear the life-enriching message and take effective action to meet your needs.

Steps to Transform Anger into a Life-Enriching Message:

1. When you feel angry, notice the sensations in your body.

2. Stop what you're doing & take a *Time In*. (See "Take *Time In*" activity in this section.)

3. Recognize that the other person is not responsible for your feelings and is not the cause of your anger.

4. Notice anger-producing thoughts (see list below), including any thoughts that the other person *should* do something. These thoughts are the cause of your anger.

   Fill in the blank with as many of these thoughts as you notice.

   I'm angry because I'm thinking that he or she should _____.

   and/or

   I'm angry because I'm telling myself that someone is doing something to me. (attacking, betraying, insulting, manipulating, etc. See list below.)

5. Sense the needs underneath the anger:

In this situation, my need for _____ *is not met.*

6. When you connect with your unmet need, how do you feel?

I feel _____ .

7. Take time to breathe with the feelings & needs. Then see if there is something you'd like to ask of yourself or of someone else to address your needs.

Anger-Producing Thoughts:

Anger-producing thoughts often pose as feelings. People say, *I feel manipulated* or *I feel insulted. Manipulated* and *insulted,* however, are not feelings; they are thoughts about what you believe others are doing to you. Identify the thoughts to get to the underlying feelings and needs:

I think you are manipulating me; when I think that thought, I'm angry!

I also feel sad and scared; I want to trust you care about me.

Topic: Life-Enriching Practices

Title: Anger Thermometer

Objective: To learn to work with anger (first recognize how it feels in the body and its range of intensity)

Type of Activity: Family discussion, individual exercise

Materials: Copies of the Anger Thermometer chart (see following page), colored pencils

Procedure:

Think about a time when you were angry. How "hot" was your anger? On your Anger Thermometer, mark the intensity of your anger or the level of "heat" you experienced in that situation. Discuss where in your body you experienced the heat and what you noticed. Think of some other times when you were angry and mark the level of heat you experienced. Use this activity to discuss the signs and stages of anger and what you can do when you notice it.

You can use colored pencils to mark the levels of heat: mild (yellow), medium (orange), hot (red).

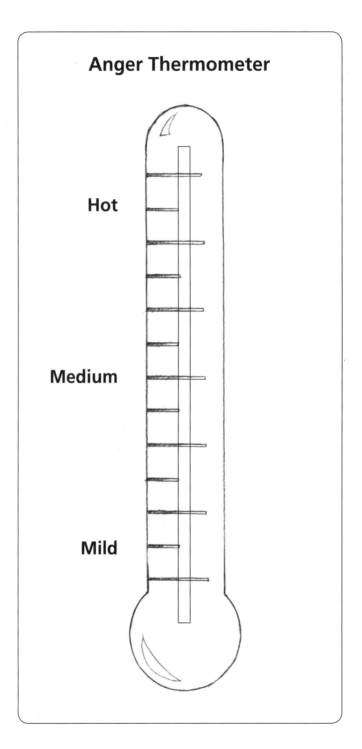

Topic: Life-Enriching Practices

Title: Daily Reminders

Objective: To keep the concepts introduced in this book
fresh in your mind

Type of Activity: Reminder and review

Materials: This book, scissors

Procedure:

1. Photocopy the following pages of reminders on different colors of paper. Enlarge to 125 percent before copying.

2. Cut out strips of paper so that each reminder is on its own strip.

3. Fold the strips and place them in a bowl.

4. Each morning, choose one of the strips of paper from the bowl. Let the message on it serve as a reminder of concepts that were introduced in the book. Go back to the key in the book if you would like a review. (Each strip includes the number of the key where more information about that reminder can be found.)

Variation: Reminder Card Deck

Photocopy the following two pages and glue the strips onto 3 x 5 inch cards to form a flashcard deck.

- Each day, choose a card from the deck to sit quietly with and think about.

- Sort the cards into two piles—concepts that you understand well and are using and concepts that you would like to be clearer about or using more.

Variation: Refrigerator Reminders

Photocopy the following pages and post them on the refrigerator door as a quick reference list of the concepts in the book.

171

Reminder Strips for "Daily Reminders"

Choose your purpose for parenting. (Key 1)	*Children (& all other people) want to be heard & understood for what is going on with them. (Key 2)*
Choose thoughts that align with your purpose. (Key 1)	*A child needs emotional safety to grow. (Key 3)*
Choose actions that align with your purpose. (Key 1)	*Your actions & reactions affect your child's emotional safety. (Key 3)*
Choose to encourage your kids' choices. (Key 1)	*See from your child's point of view. (Key 3)*
Choose ways to listen & talk that align with your purpose. (Key 1)	*Seek connection—first, last, & always. (Key 3)*
All behavior is an attempt to meet a need. (Key 2)	*To maintain safety, trust, & belonging, nurture family connections. (Key 3)*
You, your kids, & all people are always doing their best to meet needs. (Key 2)	*Giving is a fundamental human need. (Key 4)*
You are responsible for meeting your own needs. (Key 2)	*You & your children have many gifts to give. (Key 4)*
Feelings are messengers of met & unmet needs. (Key 2)	*Receive your child's gifts. (Key 4)*

Reminder Strips for "Daily Reminders"

Give your gifts freely. (Key 4)	You & your kids can co-operate to make decisions & solve problems. (Key 6)
Learn from your child's gift of liveliness. (Key 4)	There are lots of ways to do things. (Key 6)
Remember your purpose & intention for parenting. (Key 5)	You can celebrate what works. (Key 6)
Notice the flow of communication. (Key 5)	You can learn from what doesn't work. (Key 6)
Make observations free from evaluations. (Key 5)	Choose to see conflict as a problem to solve. (Key 7)
Connect with feelings & needs. (Key 5)	Trust that your needs can get met. (Key 7)
Make do-able requests. (Key 5)	Trust that needs will lead to solutions. (Key 7)
Listen with empathy. (Key 5)	You can choose to co-operate to resolve conflict or not. (Key 7)
Whatever comes up, you can handle it! (Key 6)	When you're lost, use your tools to find your way back to the No-Fault Zone. (Key 7)

Topic: Peaceful Conflict Resolution

Title: Introduction

The first two activities in this section, "Pause It!" and "Take 2," are to help your family understand conflict, and the second two activities, "Resolve Your Own Conflict" and "Giraffe Mediation," are to help you actively resolve conflicts that arise.

Giving attention to Time and Place is helpful in resolving conflicts.

Since resolving conflicts can sometimes take ten minutes and other times, several hours, it's helpful to discuss this fact up front. Convey to your children that taking the time you need to come to a satisfying resolution for everyone is something you value very much. This might involve more than one session. Make an agreement with your children about the length of each session, a time frame that everyone will be comfortable with.

To honor these peacemaking processes, some families designate a conflict resolution area in their home where family members meet when they're willing to talk. It can be a corner of the living room or a card table. You could give this place a name like The Peacemakers Corner, or Place of Respect, or Rumi's Field. When everyone is willing to meet *there*, they are already more than half way to peaceful resolutions.

Topic: Peaceful Conflict Resolution

Title: Pause It!

Objective: To understand conflict; to recognize
   needs and strategies for meeting needs

Type of Activity: Interactive

Materials: TV program or video

Procedure:

You can find conflict in every human story, and in the conflict situation you can find the needs people are wanting to meet. While watching a television program or video together, hit the pause button when the characters are experiencing conflict. During the pause, discuss what each character needs. Then brainstorm strategies that could meet everyone's needs. Then you can watch the rest of the show and see how the characters resolved the conflict. See which resolution you like the best.

Topic: Peaceful Conflict Resolution

Title: Take 2

Objective: To understand conflict; to distinguish between needs and strategies

Type of Activity: Acting, role-playing

Materials: No materials required (optional: a collection of costume items and props could add to the fun)

Procedure:

Take 1:

Act out a skit of a conflict. This could be a situation your children observed at school or at the playground or something they were involved in. Or it could be something you experienced or witnessed at work. Or you could make it up.

Discuss together: What needs was each person trying to meet? What did they do? Can you think of more effective ways to resolve the conflict?

Take 2:

Act out how these characters could shift their focus to the needs they each want to meet, and find a way to resolve the conflict.

Topic: Peaceful Conflict Resolution

Title: Resolve Your Own Conflict

Objective: To resolve conflicts without a mediator

Type of Activity: Interactive

Materials: Feelings & Needs Cards, one deck per person (see "Feelings & Needs Cards" in Topic: Giraffe & Jackal Play)

Preparation:

▪ This activity requires an ability to (1) make clear observations free of evaluation and (2) identify one's own feelings and needs. See other activities in this book for developing these skills.

▪ This activity requires that each person is able and willing to talk about the situation. If they have charged emotions, they can first do activities such as "D-Stress" (in Topic: Life-Enriching Practices) to reduce reactivity and resume interest in mutual understanding.

▪ To learn how to use this activity for resolving your own conflicts, first practice by role-playing characters in a conflict you read about or watch on a video.

Procedure:

Everyone meets at a designated table or space on the floor big enough for the number of people involved to sit and to also lay down their cards. They each have their own deck of Feelings & Needs Cards.

Step 1: Describe the Situation

Taking turns, each person makes one clear observation describing the situation, until the description seems complete to everyone.

Step 2: Express and Hear Feelings and Needs

Taking turns, each person lays down one Needs Card for a need that was not met in the situation, along with one or two Feelings Cards to express feelings they had when their need was not met.

They also express out loud the Need and the Feelings. For example: *When I waited outside the bathroom for so long while you were using it, I felt Mad because I need To Matter.*

While the one person is expressing, the other(s) are listening and can choose to reflect back the feelings and needs so the person expressing feels heard. Then it's the next person's turn to lay down a Need and Feelings.

When everyone has been heard to their satisfaction, if there is still an unresolved situation, they can brainstorm ways to resolve it to meet all the needs expressed. Or they might discuss ways to handle similar situations differently in the future.

Topic: Peaceful Conflict Resolution

Title: Giraffe Mediation

Objective: To mediate family conflicts

Type of Activity: Interactive

Materials: One Giraffe Puppet or an object to replace the puppet; one pair of Giraffe Ears (see cut outs in back of book)

Preparation: A mediator can be any age. She or he needs to have developed skills to (1) make clear observations free of evaluations, and (2) recognize and identify feelings and needs. You can practice the art of Giraffe Mediation by asking other family members to role-play characters in a hypothetical situation—or a situation you've read about or watched on TV—while you go through the following steps of mediation.

Procedure:

1. The mediator gives one person the Giraffe Puppet (or object to take the place of a puppet) and gives the other person the Giraffe Ears.

2. The mediator looks at the Giraffe speaker and says, *Facts* or *Observations.*

3. The Giraffe speaker states the facts of the situation. The mediator translates or stops the speaker if she or he starts to tell things other than facts about what happened.

4. The mediator says to the Giraffe speaker, *Feelings,* and the Giraffe speaker expresses the feelings that were triggered by what happened.

5. The mediator says to the Giraffe speaker, *Needs,* and the Giraffe speaker expresses the unmet needs that gave rise to his or her feelings.

6. The mediator says to the person wearing the Giraffe Ears, *What facts did you hear?* And the person wearing the ears responds.

7. The mediator asks the Giraffe speaker, *Is that what you meant to say?* And the Giraffe speaker responds with *Yes* or *No*. If the Giraffe speaker responds *No*, then the mediator asks the speaker to state the facts again. The mediator checks with the person wearing the ears to find out what was heard. They repeat this process until the speaker is heard to his or her satisfaction.

8. The mediator then asks the person wearing the ears, *What feelings and needs did you hear?* Then the person wearing the ears responds.

9. The mediator asks the Giraffe speaker, *Did she or he get what you said?* And the Giraffe speaker responds. If the Giraffe speaker responds *No*, then the mediator asks the speaker to state the feelings and needs again. The mediator checks with the person wearing the ears to find out what was heard. They repeat this process until the speaker is heard to his or her satisfaction.

10. The two players trade roles and props and repeat steps 2–9.

11. The mediator then asks if either party can think of a solution that would meet both of their needs.

12. If a solution is agreed upon, the mediator congratulates them.

13. If a mutually agreeable solution is not reached within the time frame allotted, the mediator schedules another time soon to continue the process.

Daily life provides a lot of opportunities to mediate, so keep puppets and ears readily available.

Topic: Giraffe & Jackal Play

Title: Giraffe & Jackal Ears

Objective: To increase choice about how to hear messages; to learn to translate Jackal messages into Giraffe

Type of Activity: Interactive, role-plays

Materials: One pair of Giraffe Ears and one pair of Jackal Ears, or a pair of each for every person (or, instead of ears, use your cupped hands)

Preparation: Copy, cut out, and assemble Giraffe Ears and Jackal Ears (optional: purchase ears from www.cnvc.org)

Facilitator reviews and understands the four ways to hear a message:

Giraffe Ears out or hands at heart, facing forward:
Hears feelings & needs of others. Empathy.

Giraffe Ears in or hands at heart, facing chest:
Hears own feelings & needs. Self-empathy.

Jackal Ears out or hands above head, facing forward:
Hears criticism & blame. Criticizes & blames others.

Jackal Ears in or hands above head, facing backwards:
Criticizes & blames oneself.

Procedure:

1. Facilitator gives a brief explanation of the four ways to hear a message. Facilitator then models the four ways by asking, *What has someone said to you that you didn't like hearing?* and responding to one message in each of the four ways, turning the ears to indicate Jackal out, Jackal in, Giraffe out, Giraffe in.

Example:

Hard-to-hear message: *You're so mean.*

Jackal out: *You're the mean one.*

Jackal in: *I'm a bad person.*

Giraffe out: *Do you feel upset because you want your needs to matter?*

Giraffe in: *I feel hurt and sad. I need understanding.*

2. Facilitator gives Jackal Ears to one person and Giraffe Ears to another person. The other family members then take turns saying a hard-to-hear message. The person with Jackal Ears responds with Jackal Ears out, then with Jackal Ears in. Then, the person with the Giraffe Ears responds with Giraffe Ears out, then Giraffe Ears in.

3. After each person has a turn, the Jackal and Giraffe Ears are passed to another person.

Variations:

▪ Everyone wears Giraffe Ears. Each member of the family writes two or three hard-to-hear messages on separate pieces of paper. All papers are folded and put in a hat. Take turns drawing and saying a message. Go around the circle and have people respond with either empathy (Giraffe Ears out) or self-empathy (Giraffe Ears in).

▪ All members of the family wear their Giraffe Ears at family meetings to support their choices and their growing abilities to think and respond in life-enriching ways.

Supplies Needed for this Project:

Two photocopy enlargements from your local photocopier center (one of the Giraffe Ears, one of the Jackal Ears)

Felt pens, crayons, colored pencils, or paints to color ears

Scissors

Glue stick

Tape

Two sheets of standard size copy paper (8.5" x 11," 20 lb)

1. Make a 200 percent copy of each ear on 11" x 17" paper using a copy machine.

2. Color ears any color you like or yellow for the giraffe and brown for the jackal.

3. Cut out ears with scissors.

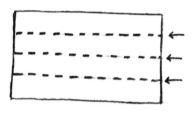

4. Take the two sheets of standard size copy paper. Fold each piece of paper in half length-wise, then in half lengthwise again. Unfold and cut into four strips. You will be using three strips for each set of ears.

5. Tape three of the strips together to make each band.

6. Use a glue stick to attach the ears to the front of each band.

7. Fit each band comfortably around the head and attach the two ends together with tape.

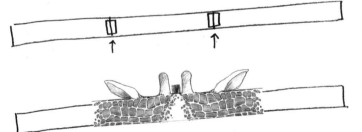

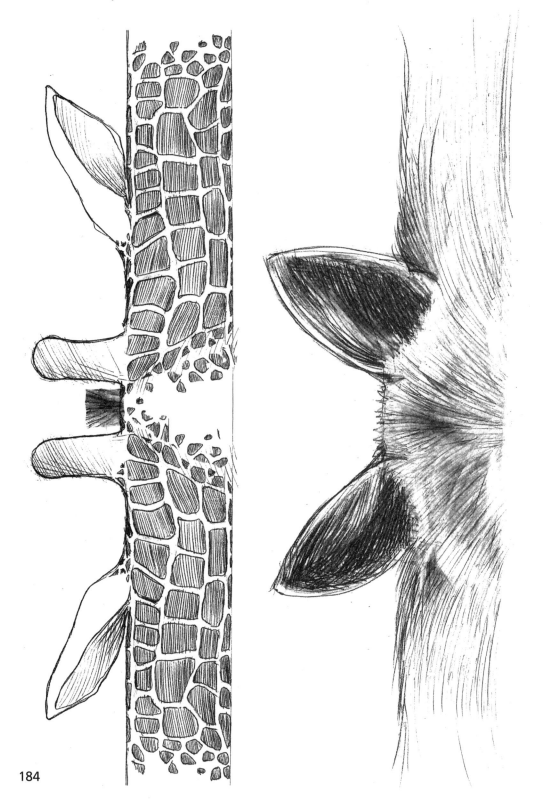

Topic: Giraffe & Jackal Play

Title: Feelings & Needs Cards

Objective: To become familiar with Feelings and Needs; to provide hands-on, visual materials to assist learning, practice empathy and self-empathy, and resolve conflicts

Type of Activity: Hands-on, interactive, with individual, paired, and group options

Materials: Feelings & Needs Card deck to cut out (and color, optional) or make copies for every family member to cut out (and color)

Introduction to *Feelings & Needs Card Deck*

Marty Mellein, our friend and a talented graphic designer, worked with us to design the deck of Feelings and Needs Cards, and then illustrated them. The illustrations and the language for feelings and needs were designed with non-readers in mind. We describe here our favorite ways to play with the cards, and we imagine you will come up with more ways to play with them. If so, we'd love to hear what they are.

For most of the activities we include here, you will need just one deck of Feelings and Needs Cards for your family. For some activities, you will want to have one deck for each family member.

Activity: *What Are My Needs?*

Spread the Needs Cards in front of you to refer to and draw from as you answer these questions:

- Think of something you did recently and ask yourself: *What need was I trying to meet?*

- Can you think of other needs you were meeting?

- Think of something else you said or did and identify the need(s) you were trying to meet.

- Can you think of anything you have said or done that was not an attempt to meet a need?

Activity: *Self-Empathy*

When you want to clarify and connect with your feelings and needs, spread the Feelings Cards and Needs Cards in front of you. Ask yourself, *What am I feeling right now?* and pick out the Feelings Cards that speak to you and place them in front of you. Then ask, *What am I needing?* and select the Needs Cards that speak to you and place them in front of you.

This activity can assist you when you need a *Time In*. (See "Take *Time In*" in Topic: Life-Enriching Practices.)

Activity: *Empathy with Cards*

To connect with your child, partner, or friend, sit down with the cards spread between you. Take turns telling about a situation in your life that you would like empathy for or understanding about. Pick out the cards that express your feelings and needs in relation to the situation and place them in front of you. You can then ask the other person to reflect your feelings and needs or make another request of them (or of yourself) to help meet your needs.

Additional Activities using the Feelings & Needs Card Deck

See the activities "Family Empathy Check-In" (Topic: Family Meetings) and "Resolve Your Own Conflict" (Topic: Peaceful Conflict Resolution) in this book.

Happy • Glad
Delighted • Cheerful

Sad • Unhappy
Disappointed • Lonely

Angry • Mad
Furious • Upset

Curious • Interested

Thankful • Grateful

Playful • Exuberant

Unsettled • Concerned
Tense

Peaceful • Content
Satisfied • Calm • Relaxed

Scared • Worried
Afraid

Excited • Enthusiastic
Energetic • Eager

Confused • Puzzled
Mixed Up • Unsure

Surprised • Shocked

Friendly • Loving
Tender • Warm

Frustrated

Community • Friends
Belonging

Play • Fun

Rest • Relaxation

To Be Heard
To Be Understood

Understanding Others
Empathy

Understanding Me
Self-Empathy

Capability • Competence
Skills

Learning • Exploration
Discovery

Choice • Autonomy Freedom

Self-Expression • Creativity

Safety • Trust

Giving • Sharing

Help • Support

Respect • To Matter
To Be Considered

Stories from the No-Fault Zone

In each of these stories and dialogues, parents celebrate the small, everyday successes that help them build their confidence and skills and give them hope that they will be able to live the love they feel for their children. These are actual stories from friends, workshop participants, and clients. We hope that they will inspire you and help you to calibrate your expectations and celebrate little steps along the way to making your home a No-Fault Zone.

Where dialogue appears, expressing statements are in ***bold italic*** and self-empathy statements are in [**bold print**] in brackets.

Saved by Self-Empathy

Our friend Sheri celebrated that she was able to quickly choose a productive and compassionate response to her child by first giving herself a moment of empathy.

Sheri was caught off-guard when she came into her living room, still panting and sweating after going for a run. As she was catching her breath, she walked to her six-year-old, Simon, to see what he was doing. At that moment, her eight-year-old son, Darin, said, with an agitated edge to his voice, ***You stink! And why are you always helping Simon and never paying attention to what I'm doing?***

She felt all the blood rush to her head and then heard herself yelling.

Before she could launch into either blaming him (*How dare you . . .*) or blaming herself (*What a horrible mom to yell at him like that!*), she caught herself at a choice point: Go into a downward spiral of anger or pause, take a breath, and check in with herself. Recognizing this choice point, she quickly took the breath and checked in:

> Real change happens in steps too small to measure and at the corner of the eye.
>
> —Stan Hodson

[Wow. When Darin said that, I felt really upset because I needed understanding. When I responded by yelling at him, I felt so sad, because I want to have respect and understanding between us.]

Notice how different her response is from self-judgment which can keep one spinning with self-denigrating thoughts like, *I shouldn't . . ., I should . . ., I'm a bad mom.* Also notice that this self-empathy didn't take long because Sheri has been practicing her communication skills for several months. The self-empathy gave her enough clarity and relief to lead her to wonder about what was going on with her son:

[When I hear and see him so upset, I'm curious what's going on.]

She was then able to be empathetic with him and check in to see what he felt and needed at that moment:

So, Darin, you seem very upset. I wonder if you need some understanding about what happened?

Darin's anger dissolved into tears, and he was able to tell his mom about something that had happened at school that was the real cause of his upset.

The Power of Loving Acceptance

This mother's pivotal choice to turn from judging her daughter to accepting her opened the door for new opportunities to connect and communicate with each other.

I found myself at a point in my relationship with my fourteen-year-old daughter that I never dreamed could be so painful. For the past year, I've noticed a steady increase in angry, reactive encounters between us. I saw behaviors that I judged as rude, selfish, lazy, and even cruel. Her response to my asking for help was negative, and as I began to insist, her reaction would be, *You twit!*

I found myself avoiding her and even recoiling from her touch. Realizing that I didn't even want my daughter to touch me was a shocking, sobering low point for me. The horrifying thought crossed my mind that maybe I didn't even love her. This was too painful to consider; however, I knew that something had to change, and I knew that it was unlikely to be her.

I realized how much I do love her, and what I wanted most was to find some way to convey that to her. I began to notice my physical responses to her behavior—how my stomach tightened, my throat constricted, and my breathing became shallow. All of this happened even before I could tell myself how *disrespectful* she was.

I decided to consciously relax my body and allow the tightened muscles to loosen, to give space to all the tight places inside. As I was able to make this shift more and more easily, the knee-jerk reactions to her behavior lost their hold on me, and I was able to stay with feelings of openness, appreciation, and affection. I saw that I had been looking to my daughter to meet my needs for respect, support, and co-operation and that what she really needed from me was loving acceptance. I saw that expecting my daughter to be a certain way was actually a demand. As she began to experience more acceptance she began to soften. She still felt free to express herself but in a kinder, more considerate way.

I'm so grateful that now, when my daughter comes into the room, even when she isn't happy, I want, first, to reach out and hug her.

Connect with Empathy and Establish Intention

This mom explained to us that, while she had not been a "big yeller," she had from time to time raised her voice while using words to "cut, shame, and blame" her kids. The experience was always upsetting for her and for her kids. She was excited to learn a way to express honestly without any blame or upset.

I'm so grateful to have been introduced to NVC. Of course, I wish I'd learned it before my sons were born, before I got married, or when I was a teenager in my parents' home. When I first discovered this new way of interacting with my sons I was learning the hard way that it was an illusion to think I could control them. It was painfully obvious to me that they were going to experiment and make choices I didn't enjoy. I realized that my relationship with them was going to depend on my ability to connect with them where they were. I have learned to trust that even when we don't agree or are very upset with each other, we can reconnect, learn from the situation, and move on, together. The connection between us has grown very strong, and it is the thing I value the most. NVC has given me the concrete skills for building and deepening it.

This story is about the night I came home from my first NVC course and was talking with my two sons, ages eleven and fifteen years old.

> Son: *Oh, brother, what course have you taken now, Mama? You're talking weird.*

I rejected my first reaction, which was to say, *I'm trying to be a better parent. Do you think you could be a little more supportive?* I chose instead to focus on them rather than take the comment as a criticism.

> Mom: *Are you guys curious and wondering what I'm up to?*

They both looked very interested, so I plunged in.

> Mom: *I'm learning a neat way to communicate that will help me say things without getting as angry as I usually do.*

They looked even more interested.

> Son: *You mean you're not going to yell anymore?*
>
> Mom: *Yeah. I'm learning ways to say what I want so that I won't get so frustrated. I can't promise I won't yell, but I think I won't be feeling as confused and frustrated so much of the time and I won't burst out yelling as much.*

Their eyes were riveted on me.

> Mom: *I'm guessing you're feeling pretty excited by that idea. You'd like to be spoken to with respect?*

Both heads nodded vigorously.

> Mom: *I would really like your help with this. I would like to hear from you when you don't like how I'm speaking to you.*

They look at each other.

> Sons (in unison): *Really?*

> Mom: *Oh, yes, because I don't enjoy yelling either, probably just as much as you don't enjoy being yelled at.*

I got that one right, too. I'm on a roll. It seemed to me that we were on a team now, talking about how great it will be when I can use my words.

> Mom: *So how was this conversation for you two?*

They hesitate. I sense they feel cautious, yet optimistic.

> Son: *This is great, Mama. Let's see what happens.*

Shift vs. Compromise

This mom was relieved and energized by the shift that occurred when she connected deeply with her son's needs.

One night I was tucking my ten-year-old son into bed. I was really exhausted. He asked me if I would stay and talk with him the way I often do. The first thing I said was **No**. I told him I was really tired and needed to get some rest. To my surprise he didn't object. I went to my room to get ready for bed, but I was telling myself how selfish I was being, and I was beating myself up for not being a *good* mom. I was telling myself I *should* stay with my son when he asks me to and that I shouldn't put my needs before his. I was thinking entirely in terms of obligation, *should*s, right, wrong, and duty. I don't know what happened, but suddenly my attention shifted to thinking about my son's needs for warmth, closeness, and connection with me, and I didn't feel tired anymore. All I wanted to do was go sit with him. I went back to his room; he was surprised and happy to see me. I was surprised that I felt fresh and was able to give him my full attention, something I'm usually unable to do because I'm preoccupied with one concern or another. That night I think we had the best and longest talk we've ever had.

Seeing Both Sides

This story demonstrates the power of honesty to create connection.

One morning when my son Peter was four years old I was making breakfast, cooking pancakes on the griddle. He called out to me from another room, *Mommy?* and I said, **WHAT!** He responded to the tone of my voice by coming into the kitchen. He looked at me with his huge blue eyes and he said, *Why do you get so impatient? I'm just asking you a question.* I said, *In that moment when you called to me, I thought breakfast was more important than answering your question. So what's more important: responding to you, or making sure that the pancakes are not too brown.* He said, *Well I do want the pancakes to be okay.*

Finding Solutions Together

Surprising and creative solutions often come when parents strategize with their kids.

When my son Douglas was four and a half, he liked to get out of bed at five in the morning to play and eat. He woke me up and wanted me to play with him and make breakfast for him. I felt irritable because I wanted the extra sleep.

One day when we were both feeling calm, we discussed the early morning situation, and we made a problem-solving book for which Douglas drew a picture and I wrote a list. In the picture that Douglas drew of me, I had flames coming out of my head. I wrote down the needs that we each had in the situation. My need was for peaceful sleeping. His needs were for playing, eating, and warmth. Together we brainstormed strategies for meeting our needs: (1) He plays with trains quietly in the next room while I continue sleeping. (2) I put cereal and milk in a place where he can reach it and he eats when he wants to. I don't know how he met his need for warmth, but perhaps the other two needs were more important to him and he found that he could meet his need for warmth later, when I get up feeling more rested and happier.

First Light-Hearted Moment in a Long Time

This story shows how important it is to notice small yet significant moments of connection.

My seventeen-year-old son is an only child. For years now both my wife and I looked to him to affirm our value as parents. Meanwhile, he has gone out of his way to resist what my wife and I want from him and for him.

The three of us went to an NVC counselor who asked us for a recent example of a situation where my wife and I thought our son had resisted and was not acting "responsively" or "responsibly." I told about asking our son to spend some time fixing a space heater for our home, and how when I came home and found that the heater wasn't repaired and asked about it, he had said that he couldn't find any instruction manual and he didn't know how to perform the task. I told the counselor that I was frustrated, irritated, and disappointed in him for not showing more resourcefulness and at least making an attempt at fixing the heater. My son said that my report sounded like the fault-finding he was so used to at home.

At that moment I had a breakthrough and I was able to make an observation of the situation, then identify my feelings and needs. I cleared my mind as best I could, sat up straight, and delivered what I thought was a nonjudgmental observation along with my feelings and needs. Then I stalled and could not think of a request to make to my son. The counselor suggested that I could simply request my son's feedback about my statement, so that's what I did. *What are you hearing me say?* I asked. However, I was very disheartened when my son said that what he heard coming through my attempt at nonjudgmental communication was still blame and fault-finding. I threw up my hands. I said, *Whoa this is really hard! Maybe I can't do this. I gave it my absolute best shot at communicating without judgment or evaluation and my son still heard judgment and blame.*

The counselor suggested that I ask my son whether he also heard my intention to use no-fault communication, so I did; and to my surprise he said that he did register my intention to change my old habits. Then he said that although he still heard blame in my communication, he also noted that the way I had just spoken to him was *WAY different than usual*, and he and I laughed at his observation. Well, that is one of the first light-hearted and simply good-hearted moments we have shared in a long time. So even though he and I did not achieve the kind of dramatic connection I was hoping for, we did connect for a moment and that connection was pretty dramatic in its own way.

The "Whining" Kids

This mom's insight about why her kids whine could help other parents who are perplexed by and don't enjoy this behavior.

A huge issue around my house has always been "whining." At the time that I experienced a shift in my perception, my children were ages four, seven, and ten years old. It seemed to me that they whined all the time. It drove me crazy. Whenever I heard that whiny sound in their voices I immediately wanted to stop whatever I was doing. Then I went to a parenting workshop away from my home where I learned that all people are ever doing is expressing their needs.

After I returned home, the first time that my daughter "whined" to me was when she was requesting something from me. I suddenly realized that she whined when she was expecting me to reject or deny her request. I also realized that she was used to having to ask for things, and she was used to me saying *No* to her requests. It became obvious to me that in our interactions my daughter was often powerless to get something that she wanted.

I immediately felt a huge wave of compassion for my daughter. I also saw how my parenting had not expressed respect for the autonomy needs of any of my children. What I earlier thought of as whining was their way of trying to be fully heard and to rebel against my lack of respect for their autonomy. When I fully realized all of this I felt regret and sadness that my relations with my children had so little trust and respect.

I talked with my children about my thoughts and realizations and let them know that I very much wanted to listen to them better and to work on growing more trust between us. When I finished, my kids looked at me as though I had come from an alien planet. My four-year-old began to cry. However, within just three weeks after my talk with them, the whining behavior had dramatically decreased, and my children and I are very much enjoying each other's company.

Chaos to Calm

Here's another example of how one person can make a shift that results in mutual satisfaction.

We had friends staying with us. It was a very chaotic situation, and I was the hostess: cooking for the umpteenth time (breakfast for fifteen people), cleaning up after that, and then preparing lunch. There was plenty of help but a lot of ongoing kitchen stress standing and cooking for long periods of time. Kimmy was age two and still nursing. In the midst of all that was going on in the kitchen, he wanted to nurse. It was really bad timing for me. I said, **Kimmy, not now. I've got things on the burner. Later.** He stood there with big eyes looking at me, not saying anything. In that moment, looking into his eyes, I experienced a shift in my needs. Before that moment it was important to me to keep everything running in the kitchen. I sat down and nursed him, and we were both content.

Helping by Choice

This mother's understanding of the difference between making demands and requests has made all the difference in how things go in her household.

I had been feeling frustrated and angry because my sixteen-year-old son was home a lot those days, but he didn't help out around the house. We had gotten into a painful routine of my asking him if he'd help with something, like vacuuming or taking out the garbage. He would either respond by making a face and saying he was busy, or he would do it begrudgingly. Neither response was satisfying and I was going around with resentment most of the time.

One day I realized that I was the one making me miserable, not him. I had an expectation that he should help out; that *should* word always gets me into trouble. Then, when he didn't help I would feel angry, and it would eat away at me for days. I realized, also, that when he heard a demand for his help, his immediate reaction was to resist or to do it with obvious resentment, which was worse for me than when he resisted.

That same day I decided to let the expectation go and see what would happen. Immediately I felt a relief. I wasn't expecting, I wasn't demanding, and all the resentment started to drop away. My chest relaxed. I got in touch with sadness because I still wanted, not only the help he could give me, but also his companionship that I enjoyed so much. I didn't stop wanting the help, but I started feeling better immediately, just doing things myself.

A few days later I had a really tight schedule and I asked if that afternoon he would be willing to pick up the dogs from the groomers. He said he had some plans and I said, *Okay, I'll do it.* An hour later he called me to say, *Mom, I can pick up the dogs.* I just said *Great, that will be a big help.*

That was the first time, in I can't remember how long, that he offered to help, and I know it's because I had in various ways stopped demanding and punishing him to make him feel guilty. I see that he wants to help because he enjoys it, not because I demand it. I sense he'll be helping around the house much more from now on, because he wants to.

I'm Not Teaching What I Thought I Was

This family had set up a reward and punishment system to get their son to brush his teeth and the mother had the following comment for the facilitator of her parenting group.

I see now how my "marking system" only got our son to obey. It was not teaching him what I really wanted him to learn, which was to take care of his health. Not to mention it helped lead to numerous struggles.

Hope for the Future

A father, with tears in his eyes, shared this with the facilitator of his NVC parenting group.

I called a bunch of parents this morning to get an empathy support team together for us parents. Last night helped me realize that the more empathy I get, the more available and present I will be for my son.

Fixing vs. Empathizing

This parent recognized what we believe is a universal truth: People are longing, above all, to be heard.

One day my daughter was languishing about, complaining about feeling lousy. I was busy with food at the kitchen counter, and as has been my longstanding automatic custom, I immediately began fixing her problem with helpful advice. Suddenly I realized she just wanted empathy for the way she was feeling in that moment!

I stopped mid-suggestion with the realization that she didn't need to be fixed—she just wanted empathy for the way she was feeling. I said as much to her and went to sit beside her. I put my arm around her to offer her a moment of conscious and deeper connection with her feelings. She responded fully, her body melting into me. She was grateful for the opportunity to feel her feelings and just be accepted for who she was at the moment. As we sat there together we felt mutual nurturing, support, respect, and gratitude.

I Really Want Him to Hear This

This is a full dialogue between a dad and his stepson Jason. It illuminates the NVC process made up of Giraffe expressing, empathy, and self-empathy.

Dad: *I found my tools in the wet grass out in front of the house. They're starting to rust. I don't know how many times I've told you how important my tools are to me, and that if you want to use them you have to take care of them. You should know better than this. I can't believe you are so irresponsible.*

Feeling his heart pounding harder and getting a little warmer than usual around his collar and in his face, Dad realizes that just talking about this situation is stimulating the anger he felt that morning.

He takes several deep breaths to calm down and relax.

Realizing that he is consumed by Jackal thoughts: *How can he be so stupid? I knew I couldn't trust him! I am never going to let him use anything of mine again!* Dad makes the choice to link his thoughts to what he feels and needs rather than his judgments about Jason. He knows that if he talks to Jason now, however, he will blow it, so he chooses to give himself empathy first.

Dad gives himself silent self-empathy.

> **Observation: [Wow! When I see things I care about left around to rust and maybe even get run over by the lawn mower . . .]**

Dad purposely practices making an observation without judgments of any kind. Judgments would direct Dad's thinking to his angry thoughts about Jason and would escalate criticism and blame and lead to more anger.

> **Feelings & Needs: [I feel irate because I need respect and consideration for my tools, especially when I use them in my work.]**

Dad knows that when he is angry he serves himself best if he quickly connects to his need.

> **Connecting with Intention:** [**I want Jason to hear me on this, and I know that if I'm really upset he won't. I also want to make sure that this incident strengthens rather than weakens our connection.**]

Dad realizes that he now has enough clarity to speak to Jason in a way that allows each of them to retain their self-respect.

> Dad: *When I find my tools left around to rust and maybe even get run over by the lawn mower, I feel really upset because I need respect and consideration for my tools, especially when I use them in my work.*
>
> *I wonder what you are hearing me say.*

> Jason: *You're upset with me and I'm never going to get to use your tools anymore.*

> Dad: *I'm really glad I checked that out with you because I was actually trying to explain something about me. I wanted you to hear how important it is to me to have respect and consideration for my tools, especially when I use them for my work.*
>
> *What did you hear me say this time?*

> Jason: *That I'm stupid cuz I can't hear what you're saying.*

Intense emotions are starting to come up for Jason. Dad decides to stop expressing himself in favor of listening for Jason's feelings and needs.

> Dad: *Hmm? It's sounding as if you're feeling discouraged about not hearing me the first time.*

> Jason: *Yeah, I never get things right. You are always on my case about something.*

> Dad: *So, it sounds as if a lot of sadness and discouragement is*

coming up about the past and other times I have talked with you. Maybe you are even feeling hopeless that things can be different between us.

Jason: *Yeah! I don't know what I have to do. I try to do my best around here. You just want me to be perfect all the time.*

Dad: *Are you feeling frustrated right now and need some understanding that you are always trying to do your best?*

Jason: *It would sure help. I get tired of being yelled at all the time.*

Dad: (gives himself empathy) [**Wow! That hits hard. I don't think I yell at him at all. I would really like more accuracy about that statement. I feel sad and upset hearing that. I need some understanding right now. Whew! It wouldn't take much for me to start yelling. But, I want to make sure Jason feels heard, so I'm going to try to stay with empathy for how he sees things.**]

Dad: *So, are you saying that it would be a relief if you could get some understanding for how hard you try to do your best?*

Jason: *Yeah! I always feel so tense around you and worried that I'm going to make a mistake or something. Like right now.*

Dad: *So just being around me brings up worries that you might make a mistake and you feel tense.*

Jason: (starts to sink back into his chair and relax) . . . *Yeah.*

Dad: *Is there anything else you would like to tell me?*

Jason: *No, not right now.*

Dad: *I'm really glad you're telling me this. And I wonder if I can tell you some things that are coming up for me right now.*

Jason: *Go ahead.*

Dad: *First I want you to know how much I appreciate your willingness to tell me what is on your mind. Then I would like you to know how sad I feel realizing that I haven't made it clear to you in the past how much your efforts around the house mean to me.*

I wonder what you are hearing me say.

Jason: *That you feel sad, or something. I didn't get the rest.*

Dad: *Yes, I feel sad and wish I had been able to tell you more often how much your efforts help around the house.*

Is what I am trying to say making more sense to you now?

Jason: *I guess so.*

Dad: *I'd like to know what you are getting from what I'm saying.*

Jason: *That you notice my help around the house and you like it.*

Dad: *Yes, I'm glad you can hear that. Thank you.*

Jason: *It's okay.*

Dad: *Would you be willing to talk a little more about the tools?*

Jason: *Okay, if it doesn't take too long.*

Dad: *Thank you. I would really like you to hear how much my tools mean to me and how scared I get when I think they might get ruined.*

Would you please tell me what you heard me say?

Jason: *That your tools mean a lot to you and you get scared when you think they might get rusty.*

Dad: *Yes. Thank you.*

I wonder whether you would be willing to help me clean up these tools right now and talk over some ways to make sure this doesn't happen again.

Jason: *I guess so.*

Dad: *Thanks. I really do appreciate your willingness to work with me on this.*

References

Carlson, Richard. *You Can Be Happy No Matter What: Five Principles Your Therapist Never Told You.* Novato, CA: New World Library, 1992.

Childre, Doc, and Deborah Rozman. *Transforming Anger: The HeartMath™ Solution for Letting Go of Rage, Frustration, and Irritation.* Oakland, CA: New Harbinger Publications, 2003.

Eisler, Riane. *The Chalice and the Blade: Our History, Our Future.* San Francisco: Harper & Row, 1987.

Goleman, Daniel. *Emotional Intelligence? Why It Can Matter More Than IQ.* New York: Bantam, 1995.

Gyatso, Tenzin (the Fourteenth Dalai Lama of Tibet). "Compassion and the Individual," excerpt from a speech given to an audience of ten thousand people in Perth, Australia, April 30, 1992. John Robert Bauer, www.john-bauer.com/dalai-lama.htm (accessed January 17, 2006).

Hodson, Victoria Kindle, and Mariaemma Willis. *Discover Your Child's Learning Style.* Roseville, CA: Prima Publishing, 1999.

Krishnamurti, J. *Freedom from the Known.* Brockwood Park, Bramdean, Hampshire, UK: Krishnamurti Foundation Trust Limited, 1969.

Lipton, Bruce H. *The Biology of Belief: Unleashing the Power of Consciousness, Matter and Miracles.* Santa Rosa, CA: Mountain of Love / Elite Books, 2005.

Mendizza, Michael, with Joseph Chilton Pearce. *Magical Parent, Magical Child: The Art of Joyful Parenting.* Berkeley, CA: North Atlantic Books; Ojai, CA: In-Joy Publications, 2003.

Pearce, Joseph Chilton. *The Biology of Transcendence: A Blueprint of the Human Spirit.* Rochester, VT: Park Street Press, 2002.

Roper, Tim, and Larissa Conradt. "Group Decision-Making in Animals." *Nature*, 421 (9 January 2003): 155–158.

Sahtouris, Elisabet. *EarthDance: Living Systems in Evolution*. N.p.: iUniverse (available at www.iuniverse.com/bookstore/ book_detail.asp?&isbn=0-595-13067-4), 2000.

———. "Skills for the Age of Sustainability: An Unprecedented Time of Opportunity." Tachi Kiuchi's Tokyo newsletter *The Bridge*, May 2002, 3.

Schore, Allan N. *Affect Regulation and the Origin of the Self: The Neurobiology of Emotional Development*. Hillsdale, NJ: Lawrence Erlbaum Associates, 1994.

Siegel, Daniel J. *The Developing Mind: How Relationships and the Brain Interact to Shape Who We Are*. New York: Guilford Press, 1999.

Siegel, Daniel J., and Mary Hartzell. *Parenting from the Inside Out: How a Deeper Self-Understanding Can Help You Raise Children Who Thrive*. New York: Penguin, Jeremy P. Tarcher, 2003.

Wink, Walter. *The Powers That Be: Theology for a New Millenium*. New York: Doubleday, 1998.

Parenting Resources

Sura Hart and Victoria Kindle Hodson offer workshops for parents, seminars for teachers, and private coaching and consulting in person and by phone.

Contact information for Sura and Victoria:
    Sura: 805.698.3332, Sura@RespectfulParents-Kids.com
    Victoria: 805.653.0261, Victoria@RespectfulParents-Kids.com
    Kindle-Hart website: www.k-hcommunication.com
    LearningSuccess™ Institute website: www.learningsuccessinstitute.com

Nonviolent Communication workshops and practice groups, including both general workshops and parent workshops, are offered around the world by trainers who work closely with and have received certification through the Center for Nonviolent Communication. (See www.cnvc.org for a list of certified trainers.) NVC workshops are also offered by many other qualified teachers who are not officially certified through CNVC. Private empathy sessions and coaching for parents are offered by NVC teachers and trainers worldwide.

For information about CNVC's "Peaceful Families, Peaceful World" project designed to establish a worldwide network of NVC support for parents, go to: www.cnvc.org/pparent.htm.

For specific information about NVC Family Camps and NVC training for parents around the world, e-mail Inbal Kashtan, "Peaceful Families, Peaceful World" coordinator, at nvcparenting@mindspring.com.

For a wealth of information on NVC, including NVC books you can order, see the website for PuddleDancer Press: www.nonviolent-communication.com.

Recommended Reading

Childre, Doc, and Deborah Rozman. *Transforming Anger: The HeartMath Solution for Letting Go of Rage, Frustration, and Irritation.* Oakland, CA: New Harbinger Publications, 2003.

Cohen, Lawrence J. *Playful Parenting.* New York: Ballantine, 2001.

Faber, Adele, and Elaine Mazlish. *How to Talk So Kids Will Listen, and How to Listen So Kids Will Talk.* New York: Avon Books, 1980.

Feinstein, Sheryl. *Secrets of the Teenage Brain: Research-Based Strategies for Reaching & Teaching Today's Adolescents.* San Diego, CA: The Brain Store, 2004.

Fritz, Robert. *The Path of Least Resistance: Learning to Become the Creative Force in Your Own Life.* New York: Fawcett Columbine / Ballantine, 1989.

Ginott, Haim. *Between Parent and Child.* New York: Avon Books, 1965.

Hart, Sura, and Victoria Kindle Hodson. *The Compassionate Classroom: Relationship Based Teaching and Learning.* Encinitas, CA: PuddleDancer Press, 2004.

Herzog, Rita and Kathy Smith. *The Mayor of Jackal Heights.* La Crescenta, CA: Center for Nonviolent Communication, 1992.

Hodson, Victoria Kindle, and Mariaemma Willis. *Discover Your Child's Learning Style.* Roseville, CA: Prima Publishing, 1999.

Institute of HeartMath. *The Inside Story: Understanding the Power of Feelings.* Boulder Creek, CA: HeartMath L.L.C., 2002.

Kabat-Zinn, Myla, and Jon Kabat-Zinn. *Everyday Blessings: The Inner Work of Mindful Parenting.* New York: Hyperion, 1997.

Kashtan, Inbal. *Parenting From Your Heart: Sharing the Gifts of Compassion, Connection, and Choice.* Encinitas, CA: PuddleDancer Press, 2003.

Kohn, Alfie. *Unconditional Parenting: Moving from Rewards and Punishments to Love and Reason.* New York: Atria Books, 2005.

Krishnamurti, J. *To Be Human*. Boston: Shambhala Publications, 2000.

Lipton, Bruce. *The Biology of Belief: Unleashing the Power of Consciousness, Matter, and Miracles*. Santa Rosa, CA: Mountain of Love / Elite Books, 2005.

Mendizza, Michael, with Joseph Chilton Pearce. *Magical Parent, Magical Child: The Art of Joyful Parenting*. Berkeley: North Atlantic Books / Ojai, CA: In-Joy Publications, 2003.

Pearce, Joseph Chilton. *The Biology of Transcendence: A Blueprint of the Human Spirit*. Rochester, VT: Park Street Press, 2002.

Rosenberg, Marshall B. *Nonviolent Communication: A Language of Life*. Encinitas, CA: PuddleDancer Press, 2003.

————. *Raising Children Compassionately: Parenting the Nonviolent Communication Way*. Encinitas, CA: PuddleDancer Press, 2000.

————. *The Surprising Purpose of Anger—Beyond Anger Management: Finding the Gift*. Encinitas, CA: PuddleDancer Press, 2005.

Siegel, Daniel J., and Mary Hartzell. *Parenting from the Inside Out: How a Deeper Self-Understanding Can Help You Raise Children Who Thrive*. New York: Penguin, Jeremy P. Tarcher, 2003.

Index

How You Can Use the NVC Process

| Clearly expressing
how **I am**
without blaming
or criticizing | Empathically receiving
how **you are**
without hearing
blame or criticism |

OBSERVATIONS

1. What I observe *(see, hear, remember, imagine, free from my evaluations)* that does or does not contribute to my well-being:

   "When I (see, hear) . . . "

1. What you observe *(see, hear, remember, imagine, free from your evaluations)* that does or does not contribute to your well-being:

   "When you see/hear . . . "

   (Sometimes dropped when offering empathy)

FEELINGS

2. How I feel *(emotion or sensation rather than thought)* in relation to what I observe:

   "I feel . . . "

2. How you feel *(emotion or sensation rather than thought)* in relation to what you observe:

   "You feel . . ."

NEEDS

3. What I need or value *(rather than a preference, or a specific action)* that causes my feelings:

   ". . . because I need/value . . . "

3. What you need or value *(rather than a preference, or a specific action)* that causes your feelings:

   ". . . because you need/value . . ."

| Clearly requesting that
which would enrich **my**
life without demanding | Empathically receiving that
which would enrich **your** life
without hearing any demand |

REQUESTS

4. The concrete actions I would like taken:

   "Would you be willing to . . . ?"

4. The concrete actions you would like taken:

   "Would you like . . . ?"

   (Sometimes dropped when offering empathy)

© Marshall Rosenberg. For more information about Marshall Rosenberg or the Center for Nonviolent Communication please call 1-818-957-9393 or visit www.CNVC.org.

Some Basic Feelings We All Have

Feelings when needs "are" fulfilled

• Amazed	• Joyous	• Comfortable	• Moved
• Confident	• Optimistic	• Eager	• Proud
• Energetic	• Relieved	• Fulfilled	• Stimulated
• Glad	• Surprised	• Hopeful	• Thankful
• Inspired	• Touched	• Intrigued	• Trustful

Feelings when needs "are not" fulfilled

• Angry	• Hopeless	• Annoyed	• Impatient
• Confused	• Irritated	• Concerned	• Lonely
• Disappointed	• Nervous	• Discouraged	• Overwhelmed
• Distressed	• Puzzled	• Embarrassed	• Reluctant
• Frustrated	• Sad	• Helpless	• Uncomfortable

 ## Some Basic Needs We All Have

Autonomy
- Choosing dreams/goals/values
- Choosing plans for fulfilling one's dreams, goals, values

Celebration
- Celebrate the creation of life and dreams fulfilled
- Celebrate losses: loved ones, dreams, etc. (mourning)

Integrity
- Authenticity • Creativity
- Meaning • Self-worth

Interdependence
- Acceptance • Appreciation
- Closeness • Community
- Consideration
- Contribute to the enrichment of life
- Emotional Safety • Empathy

Physical Nurturance
- Air • Food
- Movement, exercise
- Protection from life-threatening forms of life: viruses, bacteria, insects, predatory animals
- Rest • Sexual expression
- Shelter • Touch • Water

Play
- Fun • Laughter

Spiritual Communion
- Beauty • Harmony
- Inspiration • Order • Peace

- Honesty (the empowering honesty that enables us to learn from our limitations)
- Love • Reassurance
- Respect • Support
- Trust • Understanding

About PuddleDancer Press

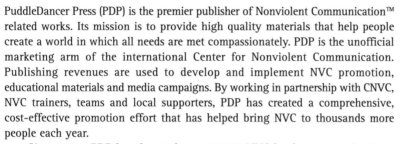

PuddleDancer Press (PDP) is the premier publisher of Nonviolent Communication™ related works. Its mission is to provide high quality materials that help people create a world in which all needs are met compassionately. PDP is the unofficial marketing arm of the international Center for Nonviolent Communication. Publishing revenues are used to develop and implement NVC promotion, educational materials and media campaigns. By working in partnership with CNVC, NVC trainers, teams and local supporters, PDP has created a comprehensive, cost-effective promotion effort that has helped bring NVC to thousands more people each year.

Since 2003, PDP has donated over 50,000 NVC books to organizations, decision-makers and individuals in need around the world. This program is supported in part by donations to CNVC, and by partnerships with like-minded organizations around the world. To ensure the continuation of this program, please make a tax-deductible donation to CNVC, earmarked to the Book Giveaway Campaign at www.CNVC.org/donation

Visit the PDP website at www.NonviolentCommunication.com to find the following resources:

- **Shop NVC** — Continue your learning—purchase our NVC titles online safely and conveniently. Find multiple-copy and package discounts, learn more about our authors and read dozens of book endorsements from renowned leaders, educators, relationship experts and more.

- **NVC Quick Connect e-Newsletter** — Sign up today to receive our monthly e-Newsletter, filled with expert articles, resources, related news and exclusive specials on NVC learning materials. Archived e-Newsletters are also available.

- **Help Share NVC** — Access hundreds of valuable tools, resources and adaptable documents to help you share NVC, form a local NVC community, coordinate NVC workshops and trainings, and promote the life-enriching benefits of NVC training to organizations and communities in your area. Sign up for our NVC Promotion e-Bulletin to get all the latest tips and tools.

- **For the Press** — Journalists and producers can access author bios and photos, recently published articles in the media, video clips and other valuable information.

- **About NVC** — Learn more about these life-changing communication skills including an overview of the 4-part process, Key Facts About NVC, benefits of the NVC process, and access to our NVC e-Newsletter and Article Archives.

PuddleDancer PRESS

For more information, please contact PuddleDancer Press at:

P.O. Box 231129 • Encinitas CA 92024
Phone: 858-759-6963 • Fax: 858-759-6967
Email: email@puddledancer.com • www.NonviolentCommunication.com

About CNVC and NVC

About CNVC

Founded in 1984 by Dr. Marshall B. Rosenberg, The Center for Nonviolent Communication (CNVC) is an international nonprofit peacemaking organization whose vision is a world where everyone's needs are met peacefully. CNVC is devoted to supporting the spread of Nonviolent Communication (NVC) around the world.

Around the globe, training in NVC is now being taught in communities, schools, prisons, mediation centers, churches, businesses, professional conferences and more. Dr. Rosenberg spends more than 250 days each year teaching NVC in some of the most impoverished, war-torn states of the world. More than 200 certified trainers and hundreds more teach NVC in 35 countries to approximately 250,000 people each year.

At CNVC we believe that NVC training is a crucial step to continue building a compassionate, peaceful society. Your tax-deductible donation will help CNVC continue to provide training in some of the most impoverished, violent corners of the world. It will also support the development and continuation of organized projects aimed at bringing NVC training to high-need geographic regions and populations.

CNVC provides many valuable resources to support the continued growth of NVC worldwide. To make a tax-deductible donation or to learn more about the resources available, visit their website at **www.CNVC.org**.

For more information, please contact CNVC at:

 PO Box 6384 • Albuqerque, NM 87197
Phone: 505-244-4041 • Fax: 505-247-0414
Email: cnvc@cnvc.org • www.cnvc.org

About NVC

From the bedroom to the boardroom, from the classroom to the war zone, Nonviolent Communication (NVC) is changing lives every day. NVC provides an easy to grasp, effective method to get to the root of violence and pain peacefully. By examining the unmet needs behind what we do or say, NVC helps reduce hostility, heal pain, and strengthen professional and personal relationships.

NVC helps us reach beneath the surface and discover what is alive and vital within us, and how all of our actions are based on human needs that we are seeking to meet. We learn to develop a vocabulary of feelings and needs that helps us more clearly express what is going on in us at any given moment. When we understand and acknowledge our needs, we develop a shared foundation for much more satisfying relationships. Join the thousands of people worldwide who have improved their relationships and their lives with this simple yet revolutionary process.

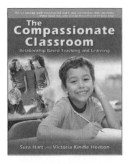

The Compassionate Classroom
Relationship Based Teaching and Learning
by Sura Hart and Victoria Kindle Hodson

$17.95 — Trade Paper 7.5x9.25 • 208pp
ISBN 13: 978-1-892005-06-9

When compassion thrives, so does learning—Learn powerful skills to create an emotionally safe learning environment where academic excellence thrives. Build trust, reduce conflict, improve cooperation and maximize the potential of each student as you create relationship-centered classrooms. This how-to guide offers customizable exercises, activities, charts and cutouts that make it easy for educators to create lesson plans for a day, a week or an entire school year. An exceptional resource for educators, homeschool parents, child care providers and mentors.

"Education is not simply about teachers covering a curriculum; it is a dance of relationships. *The Compassionate Classroom* presents both the case for teaching compassionately, and a wide range of practical tools to maximize student potential."

— **Tim Seldin**, *president, The Montessori Foundation*

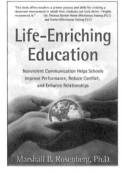

Life-Enriching Education
Nonviolent Communication Helps Schools Improve Performance, Reduce Conflict, and Enhance Relationships

by Marshall B. Rosenberg, Ph.D.

$12.95 — Trade Paper 5-3/8x8-3/8 • 192pp
ISBN 13: 978-1-892005-05-2

Filled with insight, adaptable exercises and role-plays, *Life-Enriching Education* gives educators practical skills to generate mutually respectful classroom relationships. Discover how our language and organizational structures directly impact student potential, trust, self-esteem and student enjoyment in their learning. Rediscover the joy of teaching in a classroom where each person's needs are respected!

NVC will empower you to:
- Get to the heart of classroom conflicts quickly
- Listen so students are really heard
- Maximize the individual potential of all students
- Strengthen student interest, retention and connection to their school work
- Improve trust and connection in your classroom community
- Let go of unhealthy, coercive teaching styles
- Improve classroom teamwork, efficiency and cooperation

Available from PDP, CNVC, all major bookstores and Amazon.com
Distributed by IPG: 800-888-4741

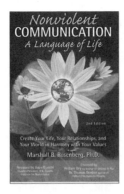

Nonviolent Communication:
A Language of Life, Second Edition

Create Your Life, Your Relationships, and Your World
in Harmony with Your Values

Marshall B. Rosenberg, Ph.D.

$17.95 – Trade Paper 6x9 • 240pp

ISBN 13: 978-1-892005-03-8

In this internationally acclaimed text, Marshall Rosenberg offers insightful stories, anecdotes, practical exercises and role-plays that will literally change your approach to communication for the better. Nonviolent Communication partners practical skills with a powerful consciousness to help us get what we want peacefully.

Discover how the language you use can strengthen your relationships, build trust, prevent or resolve conflicts peacefully, and heal pain. Over 400,000 copies of this landmark text have been sold in 20 languages around the globe.

"Nonviolent communication is a simple yet powerful methodology for communicating in a way that meets both parties' needs. This is one of the most useful books you will ever read."
— **William Ury**, co-author of *Getting to Yes* and author of *The Third Side*

"I believe the principles and techniques in this book can literally change the world, but more importantly, they can change the quality of your life with your spouse, your children, your neighbors, your coworkers and everyone else you interact with."
— **Jack Canfield**, author, *Chicken Soup for the Soul*

Nonviolent Communication
Companion Workbook

A Practical Guide for Individual,
Group, or Classroom Study

by Lucy Leu

$19.95 – Trade Paper 7x10 • 224pp
ISBN 13: 978-1-892005-04-5

Learning Nonviolent Communication has often been equated with learning a whole new language. The *NVC Companion Workbook* helps you put these powerful, effective skills into practice with chapter-by-chapter study of Rosenberg's cornerstone text, *NVC: A Language of Life*. Create a safe, supportive group learning or practice environment that nurtures the needs of each participant. Find a wealth of activities, exercises and facilitator suggestions to refine and practice this powerful communication process.

Available from PDP, CNVC, all major bookstores and Amazon.com
Distributed by IPG: 800-888-4741

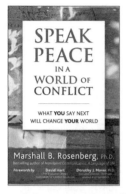

Speak Peace in a World of Conflict

What You Say Next Will Change Your World

by Marshall B. Rosenberg, Ph.D.

$15.95 — Trade Paper 5-3/8x8-3/8 • 240pp
ISBN 13: 978-1-892005-17-5

International peacemaker, mediator, and healer, Rosenberg shows you how the language you use is the key to enriching life. *Speak Peace* is filled with inspiring stories, lessons and ideas drawn from over 40 years of mediating conflicts and healing relationships in some of the most war-torn, impoverished, and violent corners of the world. Find insight, practical skills and powerful tools that will profoundly change your relationships and the course of your life for the better.

Discover how you can create an internal consciousness of peace as the first step toward effective personal, professional, and social change. Find complete chapters on the mechanics of Speaking Peace, conflict resolution, transforming business culture, transforming enemy images, addressing terrorism, transforming authoritarian structures, expressing and receiving gratitude, and social change.

Bestselling author of the internationally acclaimed,
Nonviolent Communication: A Language of Life

Being Genuine

Stop Being Nice, Start Being Real

by Thomas d'Ansembourg

$15.95 — Trade Paper 5-3/8x8-3/8 • 340pp
ISBN 13: 978-1-892005-21-2

Being Genuine brings Thomas d'Ansembourg's blockbuster French title to the English market. His work offers you a fresh new perspective on the proven skills offered in the best-selling book, *Nonviolent Communication: A Language of Life.* Drawing on his own real-life examples and stories, d'Ansembourg provides practical skills and concrete steps that allow us to safely remove the masks we wear, which prevent the intimacy and satisfaction we desire with our intimate partners, children, parents, friends, family, and colleagues.

"Through this book, we can feel Nonviolent Communication not as a formula but as a rich, meaningful way of life, both intellectually and emotionally."

— **Vicki Robin,** cofounder, Conversation Cafes,
coauthor, *Your Money or Your Life*

Based on Marshall Rosenberg's Nonviolent Communication process

Available from PDP, CNVC, all major bookstores and Amazon.com
Distributed by IPG: 800-888-4741

Peaceful Living

Daily Meditations for Living with Love, Healing, and Compassion

by Mary Mackenzie

$15.95 — Trade Paper 5x7.5 • 390pp
ISBN 13: 978-1-892005-19-9

In this gathering of wisdom, Mary Mackenzie empowers you with an intimate life map that will literally change the course of your life for the better. Each of the 366 meditations includes an inspirational quote and concrete, practical tips for integrating the daily message into your life. The learned behaviors of cynicism, resentment, and getting even are replaced with the skills of Nonviolent Communication, including recognizing one's needs and values and making choices in alignment with them.

Peaceful Living goes beyond daily affirmations, providing the skills and consciousness you need to transform relationships, heal pain, and discover the life-enriching meaning behind even the most trying situations. Begin each day centered and connected to yourself and your values. Direct the course of your life toward your deepest hopes and needs. Ground yourself in the power of compassionate, conscious living.

Eat by Choice, Not by Habit

Practical Skills for Creating a Healthy Relationship with Your Body and Food

by Sylvia Haskvitz

$8.95 — 5-3/8x8-3/8 • 128pp
ISBN 13: 978-1-892005-20-5

"Face Your Stuff, or Stuff Your Face"
– anonymous

Eating is a basic human need. But what if you are caught up in the cycles of over-consumption or emotional eating?

Using the consciousness of Nonviolent Communication, *Eat by Choice* helps you dig deeper into the emotional consciousness that underlies your eating patterns. Much more than a prescriptive fad diet, you'll learn practical strategies to develop a healthier relationship with food. Learn to enjoy the tastes, smells and sensations of healthful eating once again.

Available from PDP, CNVC, all major bookstores and Amazon.com
Distributed by IPG: 800-888-4741

Trade Booklets from PuddleDancer Press

Being Me, Loving You • *A Practical Guide to Extraordinary Relationships* **by Marshall B. Rosenberg, Ph.D.** • Discover the "how-to" of heart to heart connections strengthened by joyfully giving and receiving. 80 pp, ISBN: 1-892005-16-6 • **$6.95**

Getting Past the Pain Between Us • *Healing and Reconciliation Without Compromise* **by Marshall B. Rosenberg, Ph.D.** • Learn the healing power of listening and speaking from the heart. Skills for resolving conflicts, healing old hurts, and reconciling strained relationships. 48 pp, ISBN: 1-892005-07-7 • **$6.95**

The Heart of Social Change • *How to Make a Difference in Your World* **by Marshall B. Rosenberg, Ph.D.** • Learn how creating an internal consciousness of compassion can impact your social change efforts. 48 pp, ISBN: 1-892005-10-7 • **$6.95**

Parenting from Your Heart • *Sharing the Gifts of Compassion, Connection, and Choice* **by Inbal Kashtan** • Addresses the challenges of parenting with real-world solutions for creating family relationships that meet everyone's needs. 48 pp, ISBN: 1-892005-08-5 • **$6.95**

Practical Spirituality • *Reflections on the Spiritual Basis of Nonviolent Communication* **by Marshall B. Rosenberg, Ph.D.** • Rosenberg's views on the spiritual origins and underpinnings of NVC, and how practicing the process helps him connect to the Divine. 48 pp, ISBN: 1-892005-14-X • **$6.95**

Raising Children Compassionately • *Parenting the Nonviolent Communication Way* **by Marshall B. Rosenberg, Ph.D.** • Filled with insight and stories, this booklet will prove invaluable to parents, teachers, and others who want to nurture children and themselves. 32 pp, ISBN: 1-892005-09-3 • **$5.95**

The Surprising Purpose of Anger • *Beyond Anger Management: Finding the Gift* **by Marshall B. Rosenberg, Ph.D.** • Learn the key truths about what anger is really telling us. Use it to uncover your needs and get them met in constructive ways. 48 pp, ISBN: 1-892005-15-8 • **$6.95**

Teaching Children Compassionately • *How Students and Teachers Can Succeed with Mutual Understanding* **by Marshall B. Rosenberg, Ph.D.** • Skills for creating a successful classroom—from a keynote address and workshop given to a national conference of Montessori educators. 48 pp, ISBN: 1-892005-11-5 • **$6.95**

We Can Work It Out • *Resolving Conflicts Peacefully and Powerfully* **by Marshall B. Rosenberg, Ph.D.** • Practical suggestions for fostering empathic connection, genuine co-operation, and satisfying resolutions in even the most difficult situations. 32 pp, ISBN: 1-892005-12-3 • **$5.95**

What's Making You Angry? • *10 Steps to Transforming Anger So Everyone Wins* **by Shari Klein and Neill Gibson** • A step-by-step guide to re-focus your attention when you're angry and create outcomes that are satisfying for everyone. 32 pp, ISBN: 1-892005-13-1 • **$5.95**

Available from PDP, CNVC, all major bookstores, and Amazon.com. Distributed by IPG: 800-888-4741. For more information about these booklets or to order online, visit www.NonviolentCommunication.com.

About the Authors

Sura Hart and **Victoria Kindle Hodson** are co-authors of *The Compassionate Classroom* (PuddleDancer Press, 2004) and bring a combined 45 years of elementary teaching and parent education experience to their work. As co-founders of Kindle-Hart Communication, they've been developing and facilitating parent and teacher education workshops together for over 20 years.

Sura Hart is an internationally recognized CNVC certified Nonviolent Communication (NVC) trainer and worldwide leader in the incorporation of the NVC process in parenting and schools. She is the former director of the Healthy Family Program at Girls Incorporated, where she taught parent-child communication workshops. She designs and facilitates trainings for students, parents, teachers, and school administrators around the globe. Sura has worked with at-risk youth, creating and delivering programs on leadership, effective communication, and healthy sexuality. Sura serves as the contact person for CNVC's efforts to integrate NVC in U.S. schools.

Victoria Kindle Hodson is the co-author of the bestselling book *Discover Your Child's Learning Style*, and has been consulting with parents and conducting parenting workshops for over 25 years. She is a prominent speaker and co-director of the LearningSuccess™ Institute in Ventura, California, where parents and teachers are trained to be learning coaches and advocates for young people. Victoria holds a Bachelor's degree in education and a Master's degree in psychology with an emphasis on child development. In addition to consulting privately with families all around the country, she offers seminars in communication skills for public and private school teachers, and administrators, special education teachers, and therapists.

Sura and Victoria live and work in southern California and have been collaborating on writing projects and seminars for over 20 years. For a schedule of their upcoming seminars for parents, teachers and school administrators, visit **www.K-HCommunication.com**